Century 21
Accounting

Multicolumn Journal
11e
Working Papers
Chapters 18-24

Claudia Bienias Gilbertson, CPA
Retired
North Hennepin Community College
Brooklyn Park, Minnesota

Mark W. Lehman, CPA, CFE
Associate Professor Emeritus
Richard C. Adkerson School of Accountancy
Mississippi State University
Starkville, Mississippi

Debra Harmon Gentene, NBCT
Business Teacher
Mason High School
Mason, OH

Australia • Brazil • Mexico • Singapore • United Kingdom • United States

**Century 21 Accounting:
Multicolumn Journal, 11th Edition
Working Papers, Volume 2**

**Claudia Bienias Gilbertson,
Mark W. Lehman
Debra Harmon Gentene, NBCT**

SVP, GM Skills & Global Product Management:
Jonathan Lau

Product Director: Matthew Seeley

Product Manager: Nicole Robinson

Senior Director, Development: Marah Bellegarde

Product Development Manager: Juliet Steiner

Senior Content Developer: Darcy Scelsi

Product Assistant: Deborah Handy

Vice President, Marketing Services:
Jennifer Ann Baker

Director, Product Marketing: Trish Bobst

Marketing Manager: Abigail Hess

Senior Production Director: Wendy Troeger

Director, Production: Andrew Crouth

Senior Content Project Manager: Betty Dickson

Managing Art Director: Jack Pendleton

Media Producer: Jim Gilbert

Senior Digital Content Specialist:
Jaclyn Hermesmyer

Cover image(s): Shutterstock.com

For product information and technology assistance, contact us at **Cengage Customer & Sales Support, 1-800-354-9706.**

For permission to use material from this text or product, submit all requests online at **www.cengage.com/permissions.** Further permissions questions can be e-mailed to **permissionrequest@cengage.com.**

Library of Congress Control Number: 2018930681

Student Edition ISBN-13: 978-1-337-56554-7

Cengage
200 Pier 4 Boulevard
Boston, MA 02210
USA

Cengage is a leading provider of customized learning solutions with employees residing in nearly 40 different countries and sales in more than 125 countries around the world. Find your local representative at: **www.cengage.com.**

Cengage products are represented in Canada by Nelson Education, Ltd.

To learn more about Cengage platforms and services, register or access your online learning solution, or purchase materials for your course, visit **www.cengage.com.**

Notice to the Reader

Printed in the United States of America
Print Number: 02   Print Year: 2020

TO THE STUDENT

These *Working Papers* are to be used in the study of Chapters 18–24 of CENTURY 21 ACCOUNTING, 11E. Forms are provided for:

1. Study Guides

2. Work Together Exercises

3. On Your Own Exercises

4. Application Problems

5. Mastery Problems

6. Challenge Problems

7. Source Documents Problems

8. Reinforcement Activities 1 and 2

Printed on each page is the number of the problem in the textbook for which the form is to be used. Also shown is a specific instruction number for which the form is to be used.

You may not be required to use every form that is provided. Your teacher will tell you whether to retain or dispose of the unused pages.

The pages are perforated so they may be removed as the work required in each assignment is completed. The pages will be more easily detached if you crease the sheet along the line of perforations and then remove the sheet by pulling sideways rather than upward.

TABLE OF CONTENTS

Study Guide 18

Part One—Identifying Accounting Terms

Directions: Select the one term in Column I that best fits each definition in Column II. Print the letter identifying your choice in the Answers column.

Column I	Column II	Answers
A. bond	1. The payment of an operating expense necessary to earn revenue. (p. 552)	1. _____
B. bond issue	2. Obtaining capital by borrowing money for a period of time. (p. 552)	2. _____
C. capital expenditures	3. A bank loan agreement that provides immediate short-term access to cash. (p. 552)	3. _____
D. collateral	4. The interest rate charged to a bank's most credit worthy customers. (p. 552)	4. _____
E. cost of capital	5. Interest incurred on borrowed funds. (p. 555)	5. _____
F. debt financing	6. Expenses that are not related to a business's normal operations. (p. 555)	6. _____
G. equity financing	7. Purchases of plant assets used in the operation of a business. (p. 558)	7. _____
H. financial leverage	8. Assets pledged to a creditor to guarantee repayment of a loan. (p. 559)	8. _____
I. interest expense	9. A long-term promise to pay a specified amount on a specified date and to pay interest at stated intervals. (p. 562)	9. _____
J. issue date	10. All bonds representing the total amount of a loan. (p. 562)	10. _____
K. line of credit	11. The interest rate used to calculate periodic interest payments on a bond. (p. 562)	11. _____
L. non-operating expenses	12. Obtaining capital by issuing additional stock in a corporation. (p. 565)	12. _____
M. par value	13. A value assigned to a share of stock. (p. 565)	13. _____
N. preferred stock	14. The date on which a business issues a note, bond, or stock. (p. 565)	14. _____
O. prime interest rate	15. A class of stock that gives the shareholders preference over common shareholders in dividends along with other rights. (p. 567)	15. _____
P. revenue expenditure	16. The ratio of interest and dividend payments to the proceeds from debt and capital financing. (p. 569)	16. _____
Q. stated interest rate	17. The ability of a business to use borrowed funds to increase its earnings. (p. 571)	17. _____

Part Two—Analyzing Accounting Concepts and Practices

Directions: Place a *T* for True or an *F* for False in the Answers column to show whether each of the following statements is true or false.

1. A line of credit provides a business with immediate access to cash to pay for unexpected emergencies, such as repairs from storm damage. (p. 552) 1. _____

2. Interest rates are often based on the prime interest rate. (p. 552) 2. _____

3. A line of credit does not have to be repaid as long as the business pays its monthly interest. (p. 552) 3. _____

4. A business that is unable to pay its account when due may be asked to sign a promissory note. (p. 554) 4. _____

5. A business should sign a note for an extension of time on an account payable rather than borrow funds against a line of credit or obtain a loan. (p. 554) 5. _____

6. The portion of net income not paid as a dividend is an internal source of capital. (p. 558) 6. _____

7. A loan application should include a business plan describing how the borrowed funds will be used and how they will be repaid. (p. 558) 7. _____

8. If the borrower is unable to repay the loan, the creditor can take the collateral and sell it to pay off the debt. (p. 559) 8. _____

9. A portion of the monthly payment on a note payable reduces the outstanding loan principal. (p. 561) 9. _____

10. Bonds generally have extended terms such as 5, 10, or 20 years. (p. 562) 10. _____

11. A corporation usually sells its bonds directly to individual investors on a public securities exchange. (p. 562) 11. _____

12. The face value is the amount to be repaid at the end of the bond term. (p. 562) 12. _____

13. A corporation makes bond interest payments by writing a single check to its agent who then writes individual checks to the bondholders. (p. 563) 13. _____

14. An advantage of selling stock is that the additional capital becomes a part of a corporation's permanent capital. (p. 565) 14. _____

15. A disadvantage of selling stock is that dividends must be paid to stockholders. (p. 565) 15. _____

16. A disadvantage of selling stock is that the ownership is spread over more shares and more owners. (p. 565) 16. _____

17. Preferred stock is typically described by referring to the stock's dividend rate and par value. (p. 567) 17. _____

18. Unpaid dividends on preferred stock may have to be paid before common stockholders receive any dividends. (p. 567) 18. _____

19. A business should only raise capital if the projected increase in earnings exceeds the cost of capital. (p. 569) 19. _____

20. Debt financing is often extended for a term similar to the useful life of the assets purchased. (p. 569) 20. _____

21. The spreading of the control over the business through the issuance of new stock is known as loss of control. (p. 569) 21. _____

22. A business having a high level of debt is said to be highly leveraged. (p. 571) 22. _____

Part Three—Analyzing Transactions Recorded in Journals

Directions: In Answers Column 1, print the abbreviation for the journal in which each transaction is to be recorded. In Answers Columns 2 and 3, print the letters identifying the accounts to be debited and credited for each transaction.

GJ—General journal; **CPJ**—Cash payments journal; **CRJ**—Cash receipts journal

		Answers		
		1	**2**	**3**
Account Titles	**Transactions**	**Journal**	**Debit**	**Credit**
A. Accounts Payable	**1-2-3.** Drew cash on a line of credit. (p. 553)	1. _____	2. _____	3. _____
B. Bonds Payable	**4-5-6.** Signed a note to Stark Company for an extension of time on its account payable. (p. 554)	4. _____	5. _____	6. _____
C. Capital Stock— Common	**7-8-9.** Paid cash for the maturity value of a note. (p. 555)	7. _____	8. _____	9. _____
D. Capital Stock— Preferred	**10-11-12.** Signed a bank note. (p. 560)	10. _____	11. _____	12. _____
E. Cash	**13-14-15.** Paid cash for monthly loan payment. (p. 561)	13. _____	14. _____	15. _____
F. Interest Expense	**16-17-18.** Issued bonds. (p. 562)	16. _____	17. _____	18. _____
G. Line of Credit	**19-20-21.** Paid cash for interest on bonds. (p. 562)	19. _____	20. _____	21. _____
H. Long-Term Notes Payable	**22-23-24.** Sold common stock at par value. (p. 565)	22. _____	23. _____	24. _____
I. Paid-in Capital in Excess of Par— Common	**25-26-27.** Sold common stock at above its par value. (p. 566)	25. _____	26. _____	27. _____
J. Accounts Payable/ Stark Company	**28-29-30.** Sold preferred stock at par value. (p. 567)	28. _____	29. _____	30. _____

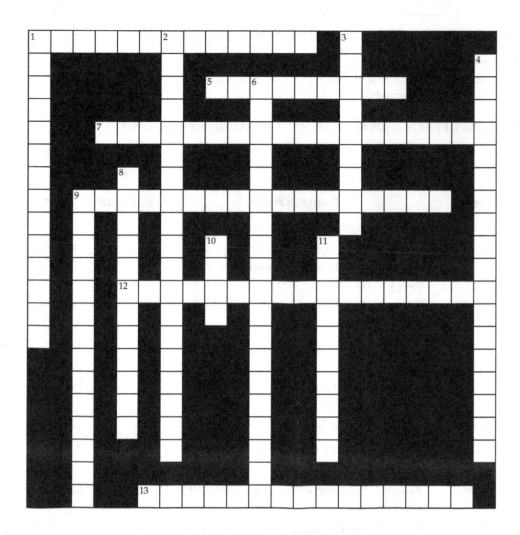

Across

1. The ratio of interest and dividend payments to the proceeds from debt and capital financing.

5. All bonds representing the total amount of a loan.

7. The interest rate used to calculate periodic interest payments on a bond.

9. The interest rate charged to a bank's most credit-worthy customers.

12. The ability of a business use borrowed funds to increase its earnings.

13. Interest accrued on borrowed funds.

Down

1. The field of accounting that identifies and measures costs.

2. Purchases of plant assets used in the operation of a business.

3. The date on which a business issues a note, bond, or stock.

4. The payment of an operating expense necessary to earn revenue.

6. An expense that is not related to a business's normal operations.

8. A bank loan agreement that provides immediate short-term access to cash.

9. A class of stock that gives preferred shareholders preference over common shareholders in dividends along with other rights.

10. A long-term promise to pay a specified amount on a specified date and to pay interest at stated intervals.

11. Assets pledged to a creditor to guarantee repayment of a loan.

18-1 WORK TOGETHER, p. 557

Journalizing entries for short-term debt

CASH RECEIPTS JOURNAL

PAGE 7

DATE	ACCOUNT TITLE	DOC. NO.	POST. REF.	GENERAL DEBIT	GENERAL CREDIT	ACCOUNTS RECEIVABLE CREDIT	SALES CREDIT	SALES TAX PAYABLE CREDIT	SALES DISCOUNT DEBIT	CASH DEBIT
										24
										25
										26

CASH PAYMENTS JOURNAL

PAGE 5

DATE	ACCOUNT TITLE	CK. NO.	POST. REF.	GENERAL DEBIT	GENERAL CREDIT	ACCOUNTS PAYABLE DEBIT	PURCHASES DISCOUNT CREDIT	CASH CREDIT
								20
								21
								22
								23

GENERAL JOURNAL

PAGE

DATE	ACCOUNT TITLE	DOC. NO.	POST. REF.	DEBIT	CREDIT
					23
					24
					25

Journalizing entries for short-term debt

CASH RECEIPTS JOURNAL

PAGE 7

				GENERAL		ACCOUNTS RECEIVABLE CREDIT	SALES CREDIT	SALES TAX PAYABLE CREDIT	SALES DISCOUNT DEBIT	CASH DEBIT
DATE	ACCOUNT TITLE	DOC. NO.	POST. REF.	DEBIT	CREDIT					

CASH PAYMENTS JOURNAL

PAGE 5

				GENERAL		ACCOUNTS PAYABLE DEBIT	PURCHASES DISCOUNT CREDIT	CASH CREDIT
DATE	ACCOUNT TITLE	CK. NO.	POST. REF.	DEBIT	CREDIT			

GENERAL JOURNAL

PAGE

DATE	ACCOUNT TITLE	DOC. NO.	POST. REF.	DEBIT	CREDIT

Name _____ Date _____ Class _____

18-2 WORK TOGETHER, p. 564

Journalizing entries for long-term debt

CASH RECEIPTS JOURNAL

PAGE 7

DATE	ACCOUNT TITLE	DOC. NO.	POST. REF.	GENERAL DEBIT (1)	GENERAL CREDIT (2)	ACCOUNTS RECEIVABLE CREDIT (3)	SALES CREDIT (4)	SALES TAX PAYABLE CREDIT (5)	SALES DISCOUNT DEBIT (6)	CASH DEBIT (7)

CASH PAYMENTS JOURNAL

PAGE 5

DATE	ACCOUNT TITLE	CK. NO.	POST. REF.	GENERAL DEBIT (1)	GENERAL CREDIT (2)	ACCOUNTS PAYABLE DEBIT (3)	PURCHASES DISCOUNT CREDIT (4)	CASH CREDIT (5)

Amount Borrowed $25,000.00
Term of Note (Months) 60
Annual Interest Rate 9%
Monthly Payment $518.96

Payment Number	Payable 1st Day of	Beginning Balance	Interest	Principal	Ending Balance
1	July	$25,000.00	$187.50	$331.46	$24,668.54
2	August	$24,668.54	$185.01	$333.95	$24,334.59
3	September	$24,334.59	$182.51	$336.45	$23,998.14
4	October	$23,998.14	$179.99	$338.97	$23,659.17
5	November	$23,659.17	$177.44	$341.52	$23,317.65
6	December	$23,317.65	$174.88	$344.08	$22,973.57
7	January	$22,973.57	$172.30	$346.66	$22,626.91
8	February	$22,626.91	$169.70	$349.26	$22,277.65
9	March	$22,277.65	$167.08	$351.88	$21,925.77

Journalizing entries for long-term debt

CASH RECEIPTS JOURNAL

PAGE 7

DATE	ACCOUNT TITLE	DOC. NO.	POST. REF.	GENERAL DEBIT	GENERAL CREDIT	ACCOUNTS RECEIVABLE CREDIT	SALES CREDIT	SALES TAX PAYABLE CREDIT	SALES DISCOUNT DEBIT	CASH DEBIT

CASH PAYMENTS JOURNAL

PAGE 5

DATE	ACCOUNT TITLE	CK. NO.	POST. REF.	GENERAL DEBIT	GENERAL CREDIT	ACCOUNTS PAYABLE DEBIT	PURCHASES DISCOUNT CREDIT	CASH CREDIT

Amount Borrowed	$32,000.00
Term of Note (Months)	48
Annual Interest Rate	7.5%
Monthly Payment	$773.72

Payment Number	Payable 1st Day of	Beginning Balance	Interest	Principal	Ending Balance
1	August	$32,000.00	$200.00	$573.72	$31,426.28
2	September	$31,426.28	$196.41	$577.31	$30,848.97
3	October	$30,848.97	$192.81	$580.91	$30,268.06
4	November	$30,268.06	$189.18	$584.54	$29,683.52
5	December	$29,683.52	$185.52	$588.20	$29,095.32
6	January	$29,095.32	$181.85	$591.87	$28,503.45
7	February	$28,503.45	$178.15	$595.57	$27,907.88
8	March	$27,907.88	$174.42	$599.30	$27,308.58
9	April	$27,308.58	$170.68	$603.04	$26,705.54

18-3 WORK TOGETHER, p. 568

Journalizing the sale of common and preferred stock

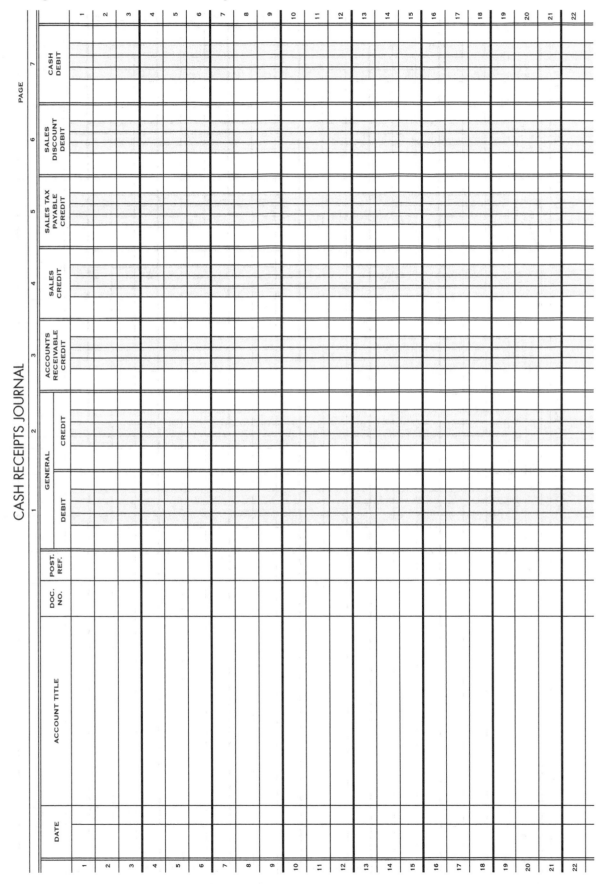

CASH RECEIPTS JOURNAL

PAGE 7

DATE	ACCOUNT TITLE	DOC. NO.	POST. REF.	GENERAL DEBIT	GENERAL CREDIT	ACCOUNTS RECEIVABLE CREDIT	SALES CREDIT	SALES TAX PAYABLE CREDIT	SALES DISCOUNT DEBIT	CASH DEBIT

Journalizing the sale of common and preferred stock

CASH RECEIPTS JOURNAL

PAGE

DATE	ACCOUNT TITLE	DOC. NO.	POST. REF.	1 GENERAL DEBIT	2 GENERAL CREDIT	3 ACCOUNTS RECEIVABLE CREDIT	4 SALES CREDIT	5 SALES TAX PAYABLE CREDIT	6 SALES DISCOUNT DEBIT	7 CASH DEBIT

18-4 WORK TOGETHER, p. 573

Analyzing the impact of financial leverage

1.

	Outcome		
	6.0%	7.0%	8.0%
Operating income			
Interest expense			
Net income (loss) before federal income tax			
Federal income tax (25%)			
Net income after federal income tax			
Investment			
Return on investment			

2.

_____

_____

_____

_____

_____

ON YOUR OWN, p. 573

Analyzing the impact of financial leverage

1.

	Outcome		
	7.6%	7.8%	8.0%
Operating income			
Interest expense			
Net income (loss) before federal income tax			
Federal income tax (25%)			
Net income after federal income tax			
Investment			
Return on investment			

2.

_____

_____

_____

_____

_____

18-1 APPLICATION PROBLEM (LO2), p. 577

Journalizing entries for short-term debt

CASH RECEIPTS JOURNAL

PAGE 7

DATE	ACCOUNT TITLE	DOC. NO.	POST. REF.	GENERAL DEBIT	GENERAL CREDIT	ACCOUNTS RECEIVABLE CREDIT	SALES CREDIT	SALES TAX PAYABLE CREDIT	SALES DISCOUNT DEBIT	CASH DEBIT
											21
											22
											23

CASH PAYMENTS JOURNAL

PAGE 5

DATE	ACCOUNT TITLE	CK. NO.	POST. REF.	GENERAL DEBIT	GENERAL CREDIT	ACCOUNTS PAYABLE DEBIT	PURCHASES DISCOUNT CREDIT	CASH CREDIT
									17
									18
									19
									20

GENERAL JOURNAL

PAGE

DATE	ACCOUNT TITLE	DOC. NO.	POST. REF.	DEBIT	CREDIT
						20
						21
						22

APPLICATION PROBLEM (LO4), p. 577

Journalizing entries for long-term debt

CASH RECEIPTS JOURNAL

PAGE 7

DATE	ACCOUNT TITLE	DOC. NO.	POST. REF.	GENERAL DEBIT	GENERAL CREDIT	ACCOUNTS RECEIVABLE CREDIT	SALES CREDIT	SALES TAX PAYABLE CREDIT	SALES DISCOUNT DEBIT	CASH DEBIT

CASH PAYMENTS JOURNAL

PAGE 5

DATE	ACCOUNT TITLE	CK. NO.	POST. REF.	GENERAL DEBIT	GENERAL CREDIT	ACCOUNTS PAYABLE DEBIT	PURCHASES DISCOUNT CREDIT	CASH CREDIT

Amount Borrowed	$16,000.00
Term of Note (Months)	72
Annual Interest Rate	7%
Monthly Payment	$272.78

Payment Number	Payable 1st Day of	Beginning Balance	Interest	Principal	Ending Balance
1	May	$16,000.00	$93.33	$179.45	$15,820.55
2	June	$15,820.55	$92.29	$180.49	$15,640.06
3	July	$15,640.06	$91.23	$181.55	$15,458.51
4	August	$15,458.51	$90.17	$182.61	$15,275.90
5	September	$15,275.90	$89.11	$183.67	$15,092.23
6	October	$15,092.23	$88.04	$184.74	$14,907.49
7	November	$14,907.49	$86.96	$185.82	$14,721.67
8	December	$14,721.67	$85.88	$186.90	$14,534.77
9	January	$14,534.77	$84.79	$187.99	$14,346.78

18-3 APPLICATION PROBLEM (LO5), p. 578

Journalizing the sale of common and preferred stock

CASH RECEIPTS JOURNAL

DATE	ACCOUNT TITLE	DOC. NO.	POST. REF.	GENERAL DEBIT	GENERAL CREDIT	ACCOUNTS RECEIVABLE CREDIT	SALES CREDIT	SALES TAX PAYABLE CREDIT	SALES DISCOUNT DEBIT	CASH DEBIT
1										
2										
3										
4										
5										
6										
7										
8										
9										
10										
11										
12										
13										
14										
15										
16										
17										
18										
19										
20										
21										
22										
23										

APPLICATION PROBLEM (LO7), p. 578

Analyzing the impact of financial leverage

1.

	Outcome		
	8.5%	9.0%	9.5%
Operating income			
Interest expense			
Net income (loss) before federal income tax			
Federal income tax (25%)			
Net income after federal income tax			
Investment			
Return on investment			

2.

_____

_____

_____

_____

_____

18-M MASTERY PROBLEM (LO2, 4, 5), p. 579

Journalizing transactions related to debt and equity financing

CASH RECEIPTS JOURNAL

PAGE _____ 7

DATE	ACCOUNT TITLE	DOC. NO.	POST. REF.	GENERAL DEBIT	GENERAL CREDIT	ACCOUNTS RECEIVABLE CREDIT	SALES CREDIT	SALES TAX PAYABLE CREDIT	SALES DISCOUNT DEBIT	CASH DEBIT

CASH PAYMENTS JOURNAL

PAGE _____ 5

DATE	ACCOUNT TITLE	CK. NO.	POST. REF.	GENERAL DEBIT	GENERAL CREDIT	ACCOUNTS PAYABLE DEBIT	PURCHASES DISCOUNT CREDIT	CASH CREDIT

GENERAL JOURNAL

PAGE _____

DATE	ACCOUNT TITLE	DOC. NO.	POST. REF.	DEBIT	CREDIT	
						1
						2
						3

Amount Borrowed	$45,000.00
Term of Note (Months)	60
Annual Interest Rate	8%
Monthly Payment	$912.44

Payment Number	Payable 1st Day of	Beginning Balance	Interest	Principal	Ending Balance
1	September	$45,000.00	$300.00	$612.44	$44,387.56
2	October	$44,387.56	$295.92	$616.52	$43,771.04
3	November	$43,771.04	$291.81	$620.63	$43,150.41
4	December	$43,150.41	$287.67	$624.77	$42,525.64
5	January	$42,525.64	$283.50	$628.94	$41,896.70
6	February	$41,896.70	$279.31	$633.13	$41,263.57
7	March	$41,263.57	$275.09	$637.35	$40,626.22
8	April	$40,626.22	$270.84	$641.60	$39,984.62
9	May	$39,984.62	$266.56	$645.88	$39,338.74

18-C CHALLENGE PROBLEM (LO7), p. 580

Selecting financing methods

1.

	Current	Debt Financing	Equity Financing	New Balances
Financial statement balances				
Line of credit	$ 2,800.00			
Notes payable	62,500.00			
Bonds payable	0.00			
Other liabilities	19,800.00			
Total liabilities	$ 85,100.00			
Stockholders' equity	146,200.00			
Total liabilities and stockholders' equity	$231,300.00			
New capital financing				
Other information				
Debt ratio	36.8%			
Shares owned by majority owners	8,000			
Total shares outstanding	12,000			
Percent of shares owned by majority owners	66.7%			

2.

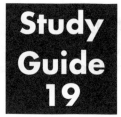

Name	Perfect Score	Your Score
Identifying Accounting Terms	14 Pts.	
Analyzing Plant Asset and Intangible Asset Transactions	20 Pts.	
Analyzing Plant Assets, Depreciation, Intangible Assets, and Amortization	14 Pts.	
Total	48 Pts.	

Part One—Identifying Accounting Terms

Directions: Select the one term in Column I that best fits each definition in Column II. Print the letter identifying your choice in the Answers column.

Column I	Column II	Answers
A. amortization	1. The ratio of the money earned on an investment relative to the amount of the investment. (p. 584)	1._____
B. accelerated depreciation	2. Land and anything attached to the land. (p. 587)	2._____
C. assessed value	3. All property not classified as real property. (p. 587)	3._____
D. declining-balance method of depreciation	4. The value of an asset determined by tax authorities for the purpose of calculating taxes. (p. 587)	4._____
E. double declining-balance method of depreciation	5. An accounting form on which a business records information about each plant asset. (p. 594)	5._____
F. gain	6. An increase in equity resulting from activity other than selling goods or services. (p. 600)	6._____
G. gain on plant assets	7. An increase in equity that results when a plant asset is sold for more than book value. (p. 600)	7._____
H. intangible asset	8. A decrease in equity resulting from activity other than selling goods or services. (p. 601)	8._____
I. loss	9. The decrease in equity that results when a plant asset is sold for less than book value. (p. 601)	9._____
J. loss on plant assets	10. Any method of depreciation that records greater depreciation expense in the early years and less depreciation expense in the later years. (p. 603)	10._____
K. personal property	11. A type of accelerated depreciation that multiplies the book value of an asset by a constant depreciation rate in some multiple of the straight-line rate. (p. 603)	11._____
L. plant asset record	12. A declining-balance rate that is two times the straight-line rate. (p. 603)	12._____
M. real property	13. An asset that does not have physical substance. (p. 607)	13._____
N. return on investment	14. The spreading of the cost of an intangible asset over its useful life. (p. 608)	14._____

Part Two—Analyzing Plant Asset and Intangible Asset Transactions

Directions: Analyze each of the following transactions into debit and credit parts. Print letters (A through L) in the proper Answers columns identifying the accounts to be debited and credited.

		Answers	
Account Titles	**Transactions**	**Debit**	**Credit**
A. Accumulated Depreciation—Office Equipment	1–2. Paid cash for new display case. (p. 585)	1._____	2._____
B. Accumulated Depreciation—Store Equipment	3–4. Paid cash for a computer for the office and a cash register for the store. (p. 586)	3._____	4._____
C. Amortization Expense	5–6. Paid cash for property taxes. (p. 587)	5._____	6._____
D. Cash	7–8. Recorded annual store equipment depreciation. (p. 596)	7._____	8._____
E. Depreciation Expense—Office Equipment	9–10. Received cash from sale of display case for book value. (p. 598)	9._____	10._____
F. Depreciation Expense—Store Equipment	11–12. Recorded a partial year's depreciation on a cash register to be sold. (p. 599)	11._____	12._____
G. Gain on Plant Assets	13–14. Received cash from sale of cash register for more than book value. (p. 600)	13._____	14._____
H. Office Equipment	15–16. Received cash from sale of a computer for less than book value. (p. 601)	15._____	16._____
I. Loss on Plant Assets	17–18. Paid cash for a patent. (p. 607)	17._____	18._____
J. Patent	19–20. Recorded annual amortization on patent. (p. 608)	19._____	20._____
K. Property Tax Expense			
L. Store Equipment			

Part Three—Analyzing Plant Assets, Depreciation, Intangible Assets, and Amortization

Directions: For each of the following items, select the choice that best completes the statement. Print the letter identifying your choice in the Answers column.

Answers

1. Recording a plant asset at its original cost is an application of the concept (A) Going Concern (B) Matching Expenses with Revenue (C) Objective Evidence (D) Historical Cost. (p. 585)

1. _____

2. A company buys a copy machine and a display case for $50,000.00. The value of the copy machine is $15,000.00. The value of the display case is $45,000.00. The amount recorded in Office Equipment for the copy machine is (A) $12,500.00 (B) $15,000.00 (C) $25,000.00 (D) $37,500.00. (p. 586)

2. _____

3. Expensing the cost of an asset over the asset's useful life is an application of the concept (A) Going Concern (B) Historical Cost (C) Matching Expenses with Revenue (D) Objective Evidence. (p. 589)

3. _____

4. The annual depreciation for a plant asset with an original cost of $2,000.00, estimated salvage value of $200.00, and estimated useful life of ten years, using the straight-line method, is (A) $200.00 (B) $2,000.00 (C) $1,800.00 (D) $180.00. (p. 589)

4. _____

5. The smallest unit of time used to calculate depreciation is (A) one month (B) half a year (C) one year (D) none of these. (p. 591)

5. _____

6. At any time, the accumulated depreciation for a plant asset owned by the company reflects (A) depreciation expense for the current year (B) total depreciation expense since the asset was purchased (C) next year's estimated depreciation expense (D) total estimated depreciation for the life of the asset. (p. 592)

6. _____

7. When a plant asset is sold with no gain or loss recorded, (A) cash received equals the book value of the asset (B) cash received is less than the book value of the asset (C) cash received is more than the book value of the asset (D) none of these. (p. 598)

7. _____

8. When a plant asset is sold and a gain is recorded, (A) cash received equals the book value of the asset (B) cash received is less than the book value of the asset (C) cash received is more than the book value of the asset (D) none of these. (p. 600)

8. _____

9. When a plant asset is sold and a loss is recorded, (A) cash received equals the book value of the asset (B) cash received is less than the book value of the asset (C) cash received is more than the book value of the asset (D) none of these. (p. 601)

9. _____

10. Charging more depreciation expense in the early years is an application of the concept of (A) Adequate Disclosure (B) Historical Cost (C) Matching Expenses with Revenue (D) Realization of Revenue. (p. 603)

10. _____

11. The declining-balance method of depreciation is calculated by (A) charging an equal amount of depreciation each year (B) subtracting the annual depreciation expense from the book value (C) multiplying the book value by a constant depreciation rate at the end of each fiscal year (D) none of the above. (p. 603)

11. _____

12. The double declining-balance method of depreciation (A) records a greater depreciation expense in the early years of an asset's useful life (B) records a lesser depreciation expense in the early years of an asset's useful life (C) slows down the recording of depreciation in the early years of an asset's useful life (D) accelerates the recording of depreciation in the later years of an asset's useful life. (p. 603)

12. _____

13. All of the following are examples of intangible assets except (A) copyrights (B) patents (C) petty cash (D) trademarks. (p. 607)

13. _____

14. A patent having a legal life of 15 years and an expected useful life of 10 years will be amortized over (A) 5 years (B) 10 years (C) 12½ years (D) 15 years. (p. 608)

14. _____

Across

5. An asset that does not have physical substance.

6. A decrease in equity resulting from activity other than selling goods or services.

7. The ratio of the money earned on an investment relative to the amount of the investment.

9. An increase in equity resulting from activity other than selling goods or services.

Down

1. All property not classified as real property.

2. An accounting form on which a business records information about each plant asset.

3. The spreading of the cost of an intangible asset over its useful life.

4. The value of an asset determined by tax authorities for the purpose of calculating taxes.

8. Land and anything attached to the land.

19-1 WORK TOGETHER, p. 588

Journalizing buying plant assets and paying property tax

CASH PAYMENTS JOURNAL

PAGE 5

				GENERAL		ACCOUNTS PAYABLE	PURCHASES DISCOUNT	CASH	
DATE	ACCOUNT TITLE	CK. NO.	POST. REF.	DEBIT	CREDIT	DEBIT	CREDIT	CREDIT	
									1
									2
									3
									4
									5
									6
									7

19-1 ON YOUR OWN, p. 588

Journalizing buying plant assets and paying property tax

CASH PAYMENTS JOURNAL

PAGE 5

				GENERAL		ACCOUNTS PAYABLE	PURCHASES DISCOUNT	CASH	
DATE	ACCOUNT TITLE	CK. NO.	POST. REF.	DEBIT	CREDIT	DEBIT	CREDIT	CREDIT	
									1
									2
									3
									4
									5
									6
									7

19-2 WORK TOGETHER, p. 593

Calculating depreciation

DEPRECIATION TABLE

Plant asset:			Estimated salvage value:	
Depreciation method:			Estimated useful life:	
Original cost:			Date bought:	

Year	Beginning Book Value	Annual Depreciation	Accumulated Depreciation	Ending Book Value

DEPRECIATION TABLE

Plant asset:			Estimated salvage value:	
Depreciation method:			Estimated useful life:	
Original cost:			Date bought:	

Year	Beginning Book Value	Annual Depreciation	Accumulated Depreciation	Ending Book Value

19-2 ON YOUR OWN, p. 593

Calculating depreciation

DEPRECIATION TABLE

Plant asset: Estimated salvage value:

Depreciation method: Estimated useful life:

Original cost: Date bought:

Year	Beginning Book Value	Annual Depreciation	Accumulated Depreciation	Ending Book Value

DEPRECIATION TABLE

Plant asset: Estimated salvage value:

Depreciation method: Estimated useful life:

Original cost: Date bought:

Year	Beginning Book Value	Annual Depreciation	Accumulated Depreciation	Ending Book Value

Journalizing depreciation

1., 2.

PLANT ASSET RECORD No. _____		General Ledger Account No. _____

Description _____ General Ledger Account _____

Date Serial
Bought _____ Number _____ Original Cost _____

Estimated
Estimated Salvage Depreciation
Useful Life _____ Value _____ Method _____

Disposed of: Discarded _____ Sold _____ Traded _____
Date _____ Disposal Amount _____

Year	Annual Depreciation Expense	Accumulated Depreciation	Ending Book Value

Continue record on back of card

19-3 **WORK TOGETHER (continued)**

PLANT ASSET RECORD No. _____		General Ledger Account No. _____

PLANT ASSET RECORD No. _____   General Ledger Account No. _____

Description _____   General Ledger Account _____

Date   Serial
Bought _____   Number _____   Original Cost _____

                                    Estimated
Estimated   Salvage   Depreciation
Useful Life _____   Value _____   Method _____

Disposed of: Discarded _____   Sold _____   Traded _____
Date _____   Disposal Amount _____

Year	Annual Depreciation Expense	Accumulated Depreciation	Ending Book Value

Continue record on back of card

3.

GENERAL JOURNAL   PAGE

	DATE	ACCOUNT TITLE	DOC. NO.	POST. REF.	DEBIT	CREDIT	
1							1
2							2
3							3
4							4
5							5

19-3 ON YOUR OWN, p. 597

Journalizing depreciation

1., 2.

PLANT ASSET RECORD No. _____   General Ledger Account No. _____

Description _____   General Ledger Account _____

Date   Serial
Bought _____   Number _____   Original Cost _____

                             Estimated
Estimated   Salvage   Depreciation
Useful Life _____   Value _____   Method _____

Disposed of: Discarded _____   Sold _____   Traded _____
Date _____   Disposal Amount _____

Year	Annual Depreciation Expense	Accumulated Depreciation	Ending Book Value

Continue record on back of card

PLANT ASSET RECORD No. _____   General Ledger Account No. _____

Description _____   General Ledger Account _____

Date   Serial
Bought _____   Number _____   Original Cost _____

                              Estimated
Estimated   Salvage   Depreciation
Useful Life _____   Value _____   Method _____

Disposed of: Discarded _____   Sold _____   Traded _____

Date _____   Disposal Amount _____

Year	Annual Depreciation Expense	Accumulated Depreciation	Ending Book Value

Continue record on back of card

19-3 **ON YOUR OWN (concluded)**

3.

GENERAL JOURNAL

PAGE _____

	DATE	ACCOUNT TITLE	DOC. NO.	POST. REF.	DEBIT	CREDIT	
1							1
2							2
3							3
4							4
5							5

1.

PLANT ASSET RECORD No. _____		General Ledger Account No. _____	

Description _____   General Ledger Account _____

Date Bought _____ Serial Number _____ Original Cost _____

Estimated Useful Life _____ Estimated Salvage Value _____ Depreciation Method _____

Disposed of: Discarded _____ Sold _____ Traded _____

Date _____   Disposal Amount _____

Year	Annual Depreciation Expense	Accumulated Depreciation	Ending Book Value

PLANT ASSET RECORD No. _____   General Ledger Account No. _____

Description _____   General Ledger Account _____

Date
Bought _____   Serial
Number _____   Original Cost _____

Estimated
Useful Life _____   Estimated
Salvage
Value _____   Depreciation
Method _____

Disposed of: Discarded _____   Sold _____ Traded _____

Date _____   Disposal Amount _____

Year	Annual Depreciation Expense	Accumulated Depreciation	Ending Book Value

Recording the disposal of plant assets

2.

GENERAL JOURNAL

PAGE

DATE	ACCOUNT TITLE	DOC. NO.	POST. REF.	DEBIT	CREDIT

3.

CASH RECEIPTS JOURNAL

PAGE

DATE	ACCOUNT TITLE	DOC. NO.	POST. REF.	GENERAL DEBIT	GENERAL CREDIT	ACCOUNTS RECEIVABLE CREDIT	SALES CREDIT	SALES TAX PAYABLE CREDIT	SALES DISCOUNT DEBIT	CASH DEBIT

19-4 ON YOUR OWN, p. 602

1.

PLANT ASSET RECORD No. _____		General Ledger Account No. _____	
Description _____		General Ledger Account _____	

Date
Bought _____   Serial
Number _____   Original Cost _____

Estimated
Useful Life _____   Estimated
Salvage
Value _____   Depreciation
Method _____

Disposed of: Discarded _____   Sold _____   Traded _____
Date _____   Disposal Amount _____

Year	Annual Depreciation Expense	Accumulated Depreciation	Ending Book Value

Continue record on back of card

PLANT ASSET RECORD No. _____		General Ledger Account No. _____

Description _____   General Ledger Account _____

Date Bought _____	Serial Number _____	Original Cost _____

Estimated Useful Life _____	Estimated Salvage Value _____	Depreciation Method _____

Disposed of: Discarded _____   Sold _____   Traded _____

Date _____   Disposal Amount _____

Year	Annual Depreciation Expense	Accumulated Depreciation	Ending Book Value

Continue record on back of card

19-4 ON YOUR OWN, p. 602

Recording the disposal of plant assets

2.

GENERAL JOURNAL

PAGE_____

DATE	ACCOUNT TITLE	DOC. NO.	POST. REF.	DEBIT	CREDIT	
						1
						2
						3
						4
						5

3.

CASH RECEIPTS JOURNAL

PAGE_____

				GENERAL		ACCOUNTS RECEIVABLE CREDIT	SALES CREDIT	SALES TAX PAYABLE CREDIT	SALES DISCOUNT DEBIT	CASH DEBIT	
DATE	ACCOUNT TITLE	DOC. NO.	POST. REF.	DEBIT	CREDIT						
											1
											2
											3
											4
											5
											6

Calculating depreciation using the double declining-balance depreciation method

DEPRECIATION TABLE

Plant asset: Estimated salvage value:

Depreciation method: Estimated useful life:

Depreciation rate: Date bought:

Original cost:

Year	Beginning Book Value	Annual Depreciation	Accumulated Depreciation	Ending Book Value

DEPRECIATION TABLE

Plant asset: Estimated salvage value:

Depreciation method: Estimated useful life:

Depreciation rate: Date bought:

Original cost:

Year	Beginning Book Value	Annual Depreciation	Accumulated Depreciation	Ending Book Value

19-5 **WORK TOGETHER (concluded)**

DEPRECIATION TABLE

Plant asset:	Estimated salvage value:
Depreciation method:	Estimated useful life:
Depreciation rate:	Date bought:
Original cost:	

Year	Beginning Book Value	Annual Depreciation	Accumulated Depreciation	Ending Book Value

Calculating depreciation using the double declining-balance depreciation method

DEPRECIATION TABLE

Plant asset: Estimated salvage value:

Depreciation method: Estimated useful life:

Depreciation rate: Date bought:

Original cost:

Year	Beginning Book Value	Annual Depreciation	Accumulated Depreciation	Ending Book Value

DEPRECIATION TABLE

Plant asset: Estimated salvage value:

Depreciation method: Estimated useful life:

Depreciation rate: Date bought:

Original cost:

Year	Beginning Book Value	Annual Depreciation	Accumulated Depreciation	Ending Book Value

19-5 ON YOUR OWN (concluded)

DEPRECIATION TABLE

Plant asset: Estimated salvage value:

Depreciation method: Estimated useful life:

Depreciation rate: Date bought:

Original cost:

Year	Beginning Book Value	Annual Depreciation	Accumulated Depreciation	Ending Book Value

Journalizing buying intangible assets and calculating amortization expense

1.

CASH PAYMENTS JOURNAL

PAGE

DATE	ACCOUNT TITLE	CK. NO.	POST. REF.	GENERAL DEBIT	GENERAL CREDIT	ACCOUNTS PAYABLE DEBIT	PURCHASES DISCOUNT CREDIT	CASH CREDIT

2.

GENERAL JOURNAL

PAGE

DATE	ACCOUNT TITLE	DOC. NO.	POST. REF.	DEBIT	CREDIT

19-6 ON YOUR OWN, p. 609

Journalizing buying intangible assets and calculating amortization expense

1.

CASH PAYMENTS JOURNAL

PAGE 5

				1 GENERAL		3 ACCOUNTS PAYABLE DEBIT	4 PURCHASES DISCOUNT CREDIT	5 CASH CREDIT
DATE	ACCOUNT TITLE	CK. NO.	POST. REF.	DEBIT	CREDIT			

2.

GENERAL JOURNAL

PAGE

DATE	ACCOUNT TITLE	DOC. NO.	POST. REF.	DEBIT	CREDIT

Journalizing buying plant assets and paying property tax

CASH PAYMENTS JOURNAL

PAGE 5

DATE	ACCOUNT TITLE	CK. NO.	POST. REF.	GENERAL DEBIT	GENERAL CREDIT	ACCOUNTS PAYABLE DEBIT	PURCHASES DISCOUNT CREDIT	CASH CREDIT
								1
								2
								3
								4
								5
								6
								7

19-2 APPLICATION PROBLEM (LO4, 5, 6), p. 613

Calculating straight-line depreciation

DEPRECIATION TABLE

Plant asset: Estimated salvage value:

Depreciation method: Estimated useful life:

Original cost: Date bought:

Year	Beginning Book Value	Annual Depreciation	Accumulated Depreciation	Ending Book Value

DEPRECIATION TABLE

Plant asset: Estimated salvage value:

Depreciation method: Estimated useful life:

Original cost: Date bought:

Year	Beginning Book Value	Annual Depreciation	Accumulated Depreciation	Ending Book Value

DEPRECIATION TABLE

Plant asset:			Estimated salvage value:	
Depreciation method:			Estimated useful life:	
Original cost:			Date bought:	

Year	Beginning Book Value	Annual Depreciation	Accumulated Depreciation	Ending Book Value

19-3.1 APPLICATION PROBLEM (LO7), p. 613

Preparing plant asset records

PLANT ASSET RECORD No. _____	General Ledger Account No. _____
Description _____	General Ledger Account _____

Date Bought _____	Serial Number _____	Original Cost _____

Estimated Useful Life _____	Estimated Salvage Value _____	Depreciation Method _____

Disposed of: Discarded _____   Sold _____   Traded _____
Date _____   Disposal Amount _____

Year	Annual Depreciation Expense	Accumulated Depreciation	Ending Book Value

Continue record on back of card

PLANT ASSET RECORD No. _____   General Ledger Account No. _____

Description _____   General Ledger Account _____

Date   Serial
Bought _____   Number _____   Original Cost _____

                        Estimated
Estimated   Salvage   Depreciation
Useful Life _____   Value _____   Method _____

Disposed of: Discarded _____   Sold _____ Traded _____
Date _____   Disposal Amount _____

Year	Annual Depreciation Expense	Accumulated Depreciation	Ending Book Value

Continue record on back of card

19-3.1 **APPLICATION PROBLEM (concluded)**

PLANT ASSET RECORD No. _____   General Ledger Account No. _____

Description _____   General Ledger Account _____

Date   Serial
Bought _____   Number _____   Original Cost _____

                              Estimated
Estimated   Salvage   Depreciation
Useful Life _____   Value _____   Method _____

Disposed of: Discarded _____   Sold _____ Traded _____
Date _____   Disposal Amount _____

Year	Annual Depreciation Expense	Accumulated Depreciation	Ending Book Value

Continue record on back of card

Journalizing annual depreciation expense

GENERAL JOURNAL

PAGE

	DATE	ACCOUNT TITLE	DOC. NO.	POST. REF.	DEBIT	CREDIT	
1							1
2							2
3							3
4							4
5							5

19-4 APPLICATION PROBLEM (LO9, 10), p. 614

Recording the disposal of plant assets

1.

PLANT ASSET RECORD No. _____   General Ledger Account No. _____

Description _____   General Ledger Account _____

Date   Serial
Bought _____   Number _____   Original Cost _____

                        Estimated
Estimated   Salvage   Depreciation
Useful Life _____   Value _____   Method _____

Disposed of: Discarded _____   Sold _____   Traded _____
Date _____   Disposal Amount _____

Year	Annual Depreciation Expense	Accumulated Depreciation	Ending Book Value

Continue record on back of card

PLANT ASSET RECORD No. _____   General Ledger Account No. _____

Description _____   General Ledger Account _____

Date   Serial
Bought _____   Number _____   Original Cost _____

                                     Estimated
Estimated   Salvage   Depreciation
Useful Life _____   Value _____   Method _____

Disposed of: Discarded _____   Sold _____ Traded _____
Date _____   Disposal Amount _____

Year	Annual Depreciation Expense	Accumulated Depreciation	Ending Book Value

Continue record on back of card

19-4 APPLICATION PROBLEM (LO9, 10), p. 614

Recording the disposal of plant assets

2.

GENERAL JOURNAL

PAGE _____

DATE	ACCOUNT TITLE	DOC. NO.	POST. REF.	DEBIT	CREDIT	
						1
						2
						3
						4
						5

3.

CASH RECEIPTS JOURNAL

PAGE _____

				GENERAL		ACCOUNTS RECEIVABLE CREDIT	SALES CREDIT	SALES TAX PAYABLE CREDIT	SALES DISCOUNT DEBIT	CASH DEBIT	
DATE	ACCOUNT TITLE	DOC. NO.	POST. REF.	DEBIT	CREDIT						
											1
											2
											3
											4
											5
											6
											7
											8
											9
											10

Calculating depreciation using the double declining-balance depreciation method

DEPRECIATION TABLE

Plant asset: Estimated salvage value:

Depreciation method: Estimated useful life:

Depreciation rate: Date bought:

Original cost:

Year	Beginning Book Value	Annual Depreciation	Accumulated Depreciation	Ending Book Value

DEPRECIATION TABLE

Plant asset: Estimated salvage value:

Depreciation method: Estimated useful life:

Depreciation rate: Date bought:

Original cost:

Year	Beginning Book Value	Annual Depreciation	Accumulated Depreciation	Ending Book Value

19-5 APPLICATION PROBLEM (concluded)

DEPRECIATION TABLE

Plant asset: Estimated salvage value:

Depreciation method: Estimated useful life:

Depreciation rate: Date bought:

Original cost:

Year	Beginning Book Value	Annual Depreciation	Accumulated Depreciation	Ending Book Value

Accounting for intangible assets

1.

CASH PAYMENTS JOURNAL

PAGE

DATE	ACCOUNT TITLE	CK. NO.	POST. REF.	GENERAL DEBIT	GENERAL CREDIT	ACCOUNTS PAYABLE DEBIT	PURCHASES DISCOUNT CREDIT	CASH CREDIT	
									1
									2
									3
									4

2.

GENERAL JOURNAL

PAGE

DATE	ACCOUNT TITLE	DOC. NO.	POST. REF.	DEBIT	CREDIT	
						1
						2
						3
						4
						5

19-M MASTERY PROBLEM (LO1–11), p. 615

Recording transactions for plant assets

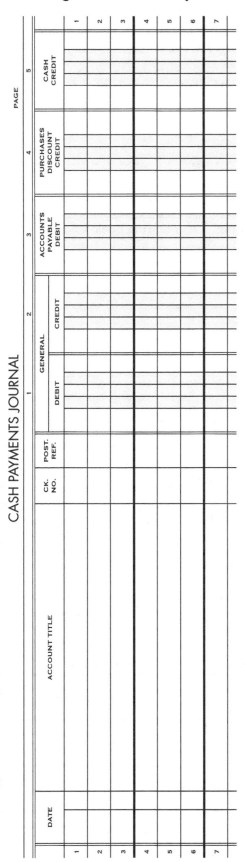

CASH PAYMENTS JOURNAL

2., 4., 6., 7.

PLANT ASSET RECORD No. _____		General Ledger Account No. _____

Description _____ General Ledger Account _____

Date   Serial
Bought _____ Number _____ Original Cost _____

                              Estimated
Estimated   Salvage   Depreciation
Useful Life _____ Value _____ Method _____

Disposed of: Discarded _____ Sold _____ Traded _____
Date _____ Disposal Amount _____

Year	Annual Depreciation Expense	Accumulated Depreciation	Ending Book Value

Continue record on back of card

PLANT ASSET RECORD No. _____		General Ledger Account No. _____

Description _____ General Ledger Account _____

Date   Serial
Bought _____ Number _____ Original Cost _____

                              Estimated
Estimated   Salvage   Depreciation
Useful Life _____ Value _____ Method _____

Disposed of: Discarded _____ Sold _____ Traded _____
Date _____ Disposal Amount _____

Year	Annual Depreciation Expense	Accumulated Depreciation	Ending Book Value

Continue record on back of card

19-M **MASTERY PROBLEM (continued)**

PLANT ASSET RECORD No. _____		General Ledger Account No. _____	

Description _____ General Ledger Account _____

Date
Bought _____ Serial Number _____ Original Cost _____

Estimated Useful Life _____ Estimated Salvage Value _____ Depreciation Method _____

Disposed of:	Discarded _____	Sold _____	Traded _____

Date _____ Disposal Amount _____

Year	Annual Depreciation Expense	Accumulated Depreciation	Ending Book Value
Continue record on back of card			

3.

DEPRECIATION TABLE

Plant asset: _____ Estimated salvage value: _____

Depreciation method: _____ Estimated useful life: _____

Original cost: _____ Date bought: _____

Year	Beginning Book Value	Annual Depreciation	Accumulated Depreciation	Ending Book Value

DEPRECIATION TABLE

Plant asset: Estimated salvage value:

Depreciation method: Estimated useful life:

Depreciation rate: Date bought:

Original cost:

Year	Beginning Book Value	Annual Depreciation	Accumulated Depreciation	Ending Book Value

DEPRECIATION TABLE

Plant asset: Estimated salvage value:

Depreciation method: Estimated useful life:

Original cost: Date bought:

Year	Beginning Book Value	Annual Depreciation	Accumulated Depreciation	Ending Book Value

19-M MASTERY PROBLEM (concluded)

5.

CASH RECEIPTS JOURNAL

PAGE 7

| | DOC. NO. | POST. REF. | GENERAL | | ACCOUNTS RECEIVABLE CREDIT | SALES CREDIT | SALES TAX PAYABLE CREDIT | SALES DISCOUNT DEBIT | CASH DEBIT |
DATE	ACCOUNT TITLE			DEBIT	CREDIT					
			1	2	3	4	5	6	7
1										
2										
3										
4										
5										
6										
7										

GENERAL JOURNAL

PAGE

DATE	ACCOUNT TITLE	DOC. NO.	POST. REF.	DEBIT	CREDIT
				1	
				2	
				3	
				4	
				5	
				6	
				7	
				8	

Calculating a partial year's depreciation using the double declining-balance method

DEPRECIATION TABLE

Plant asset: Estimated salvage value:

Depreciation method: Estimated useful life:

Depreciation rate: Date bought:

Original cost:

Year	Beginning Book Value	Annual Depreciation	Accumulated Depreciation	Ending Book Value

DEPRECIATION TABLE

Plant asset: Estimated salvage value:

Depreciation method: Estimated useful life:

Depreciation rate: Date bought:

Original cost:

Year	Beginning Book Value	Annual Depreciation	Accumulated Depreciation	Ending Book Value

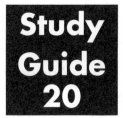

Study Guide 20

Name	Perfect Score	Your Score
Identifying Accounting Terms	9 Pts.	
Analyzing Inventory Systems	10 Pts.	
Analyzing LIFO, FIFO, and Weighted-Average Methods	12 Pts.	
Total	31 Pts.	

Part One—Identifying Accounting Terms

Directions: Select the one term in Column I that best fits each definition in Column II. Print the letter identifying your choice in the Answers column.

Column I	Column II	Answers
A. first-in, first-out inventory costing method (FIFO)	**1.** A form used during a physical inventory to record information about each item of merchandise on hand. (p. 622)	1. _____
B. gross profit method of estimating inventory	**2.** A form used to show the kind of merchandise, quantity received, quantity sold, and balance on hand. (p. 623)	2. _____
C. inventory record	**3.** A file of stock records for all merchandise on hand. (p. 623)	3. _____
D. last-in, first-out inventory costing method (LIFO)	**4.** Using the cost of merchandise purchased first to calculate the cost of merchandise sold first. (p. 626)	4. _____
E. lower of cost or market	**5.** Using the cost of merchandise purchased last to calculate the cost of merchandise sold first. (p. 627)	5. _____
F. market value	**6.** Using the average cost of beginning inventory plus merchandise purchased during a fiscal period to calculate the cost of merchandise sold. (p. 628)	6. _____
G. stock ledger	**7.** The amount that must be paid to replace an asset. (p. 630)	7. _____
H. stock record	**8.** Using the lower of cost or market value to calculate the cost of ending merchandise inventory. (p. 630)	8. _____
I. weighted-average inventory costing method	**9.** Estimating inventory by using the previous year's percentage of gross profit on operations. (p. 633)	9. _____

Part Two—Analyzing Inventory Systems

Directions: Place a T for True or an F for False in the Answers column to show whether each of the following statements is true or false.

Answers

1. Merchandise inventory on hand is typically the largest asset of a merchandising business. (p. 620)

   1. _____

2. The only financial statement on which the value of merchandise on hand is reported is the income statement. (p. 620)

   2. _____

3. The net income of a business can be increased by maintaining a merchandise inventory that is larger than needed. (p. 621)

   3. _____

4. A merchandise inventory evaluated at the end of a fiscal period is known as a periodic inventory. (p. 621)

   4. _____

5. A periodic inventory conducted by counting, weighing, or measuring items of merchandise on hand is also called a physical inventory. (p. 622)

   5. _____

6. A minimum inventory balance is the amount of merchandise that will typically last until ordered merchandise can be received from vendors. (p. 623)

   6. _____

7. A perpetual inventory system provides day-to-day information about the quality of merchandise on hand. (p. 623)

   7. _____

8. Many merchandising businesses use a POS terminal to read UPC codes on products and update the stock ledger. (p. 623)

   8. _____

9. The first-in, first-out method is used to determine the quantity of each type of merchandise on hand. (p. 626)

   9. _____

10. The gross profit method makes it possible to prepare monthly income statements without taking a physical inventory. (p. 633)

    10. _____

Part Three—Analyzing LIFO, FIFO and Weighted-Average Methods

Directions: For each of the following items, select the choice that best completes the statement. Print the letter identifying your choice in the Answers column.

Answers

1. Calculating an accurate inventory cost to assure that gross profit and net income are reported correctly on the income statement is an application of the accounting concept (A) Consistent Reporting (B) Perpetual Inventory (C) Adequate Disclosure (D) none of the above. (p. 620)

1. _____

2. When the FIFO method is used, cost of merchandise sold is valued at (A) the average cost (B) the most recent cost (C) the earliest cost (D) none of these. (p. 626)

2. _____

3. The FIFO method is based on the assumption that the merchandise purchased first is the merchandise (A) sold first (B) sold last (C) in ending inventory (D) none of these. (p. 626)

3. _____

4. When the FIFO method is used, cost of merchandise sold is priced at (A) the average cost (B) the earliest cost (C) the most recent cost (D) none of these. (p. 626)

4. _____

5. Using an inventory costing method to charge costs of merchandise against current revenue is an application of the accounting concept (A) Adequate Disclosure (B) Consistent Reporting (C) Matching Expenses with Revenue (D) none of these. (p. 627)

5. _____

6. The LIFO method is based on the assumption that the merchandise purchased first is the merchandise (A) sold first (B) sold last (C) that cost the most (D) none of these. (p. 627)

6. _____

7. When the LIFO method is used, ending inventory units are valued at the (A) average cost (B) earliest cost (C) most recent cost (D) none of these. (p. 627)

7. _____

8. The weighted-average method is based on the assumption that the cost of merchandise sold should be calculated using the (A) average cost per unit of beginning inventory (B) average cost of ending inventory (C) average cost of beginning inventory plus purchases during the fiscal period (D) average cost of ending inventory plus purchases during the fiscal period. (p. 628)

8. _____

9. When the weighted-average method is used, units sold are valued at (A) the earliest cost (B) the most recent cost (C) the average cost (D) none of these. (p. 628)

9. _____

10. A business that uses the same inventory costing method for all fiscal periods is applying the accounting concept (A) Consistent Reporting (B) Accounting Period Cycle (C) Perpetual Inventory (D) Adequate Disclosure. (p. 630)

10. _____

11. In a year of rising costs, the inventory method that gives the highest possible value for ending inventory is (A) FIFO (B) LIFO (C) weighted-average (D) gross profit. (p. 630)

11. _____

12. In a year of falling costs, the inventory method that gives the highest possible value for ending inventory is (A) weighted-average (B) LIFO (C) FIFO (D) gross profit. (p. 630)

12. _____

Across

3. A form used to show the kind of merchandise, quantity received, quantity sold, and balance on hand.

5. Allocating factory overhead based on the level of major activities.

6. A form used during a physical inventory to record information about each item of merchandise on hand.

Down

1. The amount that must be paid to replace an asset.

2. A file of stock records for all merchandise on hand.

4. All expenses other than direct materials and direct labor that apply to making products.

20-1 WORK TOGETHER, p. 625

Preparing a stock record

1.

STOCK RECORD

Description Soaker Hose   Stock No. GL764-3
Reorder 40   Minimum 10   Location Bin 41

1	2	3	4	5	6	7
INCREASES			DECREASES			BALANCE
DATE	PURCHASE INVOICE NO.	QUANTITY	DATE	SALES INVOICE NO.	QUANTITY	QUANTITY
			Sept. 15	715	2	12

20-1 ON YOUR OWN, p. 625

Preparing a stock record

1.

STOCK RECORD

Description O-rings   Stock No. 7461XG
Reorder 150   Minimum 20   Location Rack 22

1	2	3	4	5	6	7
INCREASES			DECREASES			BALANCE
DATE	PURCHASE INVOICE NO.	QUANTITY	DATE	SALES INVOICE NO.	QUANTITY	QUANTITY
			Oct. 30	215	15	65

Determining the cost of inventory using the FIFO, LIFO, and weighted-average inventory costing methods

FIFO Method

Purchase Dates	Units Purchased	Unit Cost	Total Cost	FIFO Units on Hand	FIFO Cost
January 1, beginning inventory	14	$32.00	$ 448.00		
March 29, purchases	9	34.00	306.00		
May 6, purchases	10	36.00	360.00		
August 28, purchases	8	38.00	304.00		
November 8, purchases	9	40.00	360.00		
Totals	50		$1,778.00		

LIFO Method

Purchase Dates	Units Purchased	Unit Cost	Total Cost	LIFO Units on Hand	LIFO Cost
January 1, beginning inventory	14	$32.00	$ 448.00		
March 29, purchases	9	34.00	306.00		
May 6, purchases	10	36.00	360.00		
August 28, purchases	8	38.00	304.00		
November 8, purchases	9	40.00	360.00		
Totals	50		$1,778.00		

Weighted-Average Method

Purchases			Total Cost
Date	Units	Unit Cost	
January 1, beginning inventory	14	$32.00	
March 29, purchases	9	34.00	
May 6, purchases	10	36.00	
August 28, purchases	8	38.00	
November 8, purchases	9	40.00	
Totals	50		

Name _____ Date _____ Class _____

20-2 ON YOUR OWN, p. 632

Determining the cost of inventory using the FIFO, LIFO, and weighted-average inventory costing methods

FIFO Method

Purchase Dates	Units Purchased	Unit Cost	Total Cost	FIFO Units on Hand	FIFO Cost
January 1, beginning inventory	18	$3.60	$ 64.80		
April 9, purchases	12	3.70	44.40		
June 12, purchases	14	3.80	53.20		
September 22, purchases	15	4.00	60.00		
November 20, purchases	16	4.10	65.60		
Totals	75		$288.00		

LIFO Method

Purchase Dates	Units Purchased	Unit Cost	Total Cost	LIFO Units on Hand	LIFO Cost
January 1, beginning inventory	18	$3.60	$ 64.80		
April 9, purchases	12	3.70	44.40		
June 12, purchases	14	3.80	53.20		
September 22, purchases	15	4.00	60.00		
November 20, purchases	16	4.10	65.60		
Totals	75		$288.00		

Weighted-Average Method

Purchases			Total Cost
Date	Units	Unit Cost	
January 1, beginning inventory	18	$3.60	
April 9, purchases	12	3.70	
June 12, purchases	14	3.80	
September 22, purchases	15	4.00	
November 20, purchases	16	4.10	
Totals	75		

Chapter 20 Accounting for Inventory • **71**

© 2019 Cengage®. May not be scanned, copied or duplicated, or posted to a publicly accessible website, in whole or in part.

Estimating ending inventory using the gross profit method

1.

STEP 1:

Beginning inventory, June 1...

Plus   net purchases for June 1 to June 30 .... _____

Equals   cost of merchandise available for sale.. _____

STEP 2:

Net sales for June 1 to June 30...

Times   previous year's gross profit percentage... _____

Equals   estimated gross profit on operations... _____

STEP 3:

Net sales for June 1 to June 30...

Less   estimated gross profit on operations.. _____

Equals   estimated cost of merchandise sold... _____

STEP 4:

Cost of merchandise available for sale..

Less   estimated cost of merchandise sold.. _____

Equals   estimated ending merchandise inventory .... _____

2.

Goldsmith Company

Income Statement

For Month Ended June 30, 20--

			% OF NET SALES
Operating Revenue:			
Net Sales			
Cost of Merchandise Sold:			
Beginning Inventory, June 1			
Net Purchases			
Merchandise Available for Sale			
Less Estimated Ending Inventory, June 30			
Cost of Merchandise Sold			
Gross Profit on Operations			
Operating Expenses			
Net Income			

20-3 ON YOUR OWN, p. 635

Estimating ending inventory using the gross profit method

1.

STEP 1:
Beginning inventory, April 1 ....
Plus net purchases for April 1 to April 30.. _____
Equals cost of merchandise available for sale.. _____
STEP 2:
Net sales for April 1 to April 30 ....
Times previous year's gross profit percentage... _____
Equals estimated gross profit on operations... _____
STEP 3:
Net sales for April 1 to April 30 ....
Less estimated gross profit on operations.. _____
Equals estimated cost of merchandise sold.. _____
STEP 4:
Cost of merchandise available for sale...
Less estimated cost of merchandise sold.. _____
Equals estimated ending merchandise inventory .... _____

2.

Leah Enterprises

Income Statement

For Month Ended April 30, 20--

					% OF NET SALES
Operating Revenue:					
Net Sales					
Cost of Merchandise Sold:					
Beginning Inventory, April 1					
Net Purchases					
Merchandise Available for Sale					
Less Estimated Ending Inventory, April 30					
Cost of Merchandise Sold					
Gross Profit on Operations					
Operating Expenses					
Net Income					

Preparing a stock record

STOCK RECORD

Description   42-inch Flat-Screen Television   Stock No. 891DC-5

Reorder   10   Minimum   4   Location   Shelf B17

1	2	3	4	5	6	7
INCREASES			DECREASES			BALANCE
DATE	PURCHASE INVOICE NO.	QUANTITY	DATE	SALES INVOICE NO.	QUANTITY	QUANTITY
			Jan. 3	872	1	7

20-2 APPLICATION PROBLEM (LO2, 3, 4), p. 639

Determining the cost of inventory using the FIFO, LIFO, and weighted-average inventory costing methods

FIFO Method

Purchase Dates	Units Purchased	Unit Cost	Total Cost	FIFO Units on Hand	FIFO Cost
January 1, beginning inventory	100	$4.00	$ 400.00		
March 13, purchases	88	4.10	360.80		
June 8, purchases	90	4.25	382.50		
September 16, purchases	94	4.30	404.20		
December 22, purchases	98	4.40	431.20		
Totals	470		$1,978.70		

LIFO Method

Purchase Dates	Units Purchased	Unit Cost	Total Cost	LIFO Units on Hand	LIFO Cost
January 1, beginning inventory	100	$4.00	$ 400.00		
March 13, purchases	88	4.10	360.80		
June 8, purchases	90	4.25	382.50		
September 16, purchases	94	4.30	404.20		
December 22, purchases	98	4.40	431.20		
Totals	470		$1,978.70		

Weighted-Average Method

Purchases			Total Cost
Date	Units	Unit Cost	
January 1, beginning inventory	100	$4.00	
March 13, purchases	88	4.10	
June 8, purchases	90	4.25	
September 16, purchases	94	4.30	
December 22, purchases	98	4.40	
Totals	470		

Estimating ending inventory using the gross profit method

1.

STEP 1:

Beginning inventory, March 1 ....

Plus net purchases for March 1 to March 31 ....

Equals cost of merchandise available for sale .... _____

STEP 2:

Net sales for March 1 to March 31 ....

Times previous year's gross profit percentage ....

Equals estimated gross profit on operations .... _____

STEP 3:

Net sales for March 1 to March 31 ....

Less estimated gross profit on operations ....

Equals estimated cost of merchandise sold .... _____

STEP 4:

Cost of merchandise available for sale ....

Less estimated cost of merchandise sold ....

Equals estimated ending merchandise inventory .... _____

2.

Lee Industries

Income Statement

For Month Ended March 31, 20--

			% OF NET SALES
Operating Revenue:			
Net Sales			
Cost of Merchandise Sold:			
Beginning Inventory, March 1			
Net Purchases			
Merchandise Available for Sale			
Less Estimated Ending Inventory, March 31			
Cost of Merchandise Sold			
Gross Profit on Operations			
Operating Expenses			
Net Income			

20-M MASTERY PROBLEM (LO2, 3, 4), p. 640

Determining the cost of inventory using the FIFO, LIFO, and weighted-average inventory costing methods

1.

STOCK RECORD						

Description Print Cartridge   Stock No. 120-HP
Reorder 40   Minimum 20   Location Bin 27-X

1	2	3	4	5	6	7
INCREASES			DECREASES			BALANCE
DATE	PURCHASE INVOICE NO.	QUANTITY	DATE	SALES INVOICE NO.	QUANTITY	QUANTITY
			Jan. 1		16	16

2. FIFO Method

Purchase Dates	Units Purchased	Unit Cost	Total Cost	FIFO Units on Hand	FIFO Cost
January 1, beginning inventory	16	$ 9.96	$ 159.36		
January 6, purchases					
April 14, purchases					
August 3, purchases					
December 12, purchases					
Totals					

LIFO Method

Purchase Dates	Units Purchased	Unit Cost	Total Cost	LIFO Units on Hand	LIFO Cost
January 1, beginning inventory	16	$ 9.96	$ 159.36		
January 6, purchases					
April 14, purchases					
August 3, purchases					
December 12, purchases					
Totals					

Weighted-Average Method

Date	Units	Unit Cost	Total Cost
January 1, beginning inventory	16	$ 9.96	
January 6, purchases			
April 14, purchases			
August 3, purchases			
December 12, purchases			
Totals			

20-M **MASTERY PROBLEM (concluded)**

3.

	FIFO	LIFO	Weighted-Average
Merchandise Available for Sale			
Ending Inventory			
Cost of Merchandise Sold			

Lowest Cost of Merchandise Sold:

Determining the cost of merchandise inventory destroyed in a fire

1.

Gross profit on operations ....

Divided by net sales ....

Equals gross profit percentage of net sales (prior year) .... _____

2.

STEP 1:

Beginning inventory, May 1..

Plus net purchases for May 1 to May 12 ....

Equals cost of merchandise available for sale.. _____

STEP 2:

Net sales for May 1 to May 12..

Times previous year's gross profit percentage...

Equals estimated gross profit on operations.. _____

STEP 3:

Net sales for May 1 to May 12..

Less estimated gross profit on operations..

Equals estimated cost of merchandise sold... _____

STEP 4:

Cost of merchandise available for sale..

Less estimated cost of merchandise sold...

Equals estimated ending merchandise inventory .... _____

3.

Estimated merchandise inventory, May 12 ....

Less cost of merchandise inventory not destroyed ....

Equals estimated cost of merchandise inventory destroyed... _____

20-C **CHALLENGE PROBLEM (continued)**

4.

Albertson Painting Company

Income Statement

For the Period May 1 to May 12, 20--

			% OF NET SALES
Operating Revenue:			
Net Sales			
Cost of Merchandise Sold:			
Beginning Inventory, May 1			
Net Purchases			
Merchandise Available for Sale			
Less Estimated Ending Inventory, May 12			
Cost of Merchandise Sold			
Gross Profit on Operations			
Operating Expenses			
Net Income			

REINFORCEMENT ACTIVITY 3, Part A, p. 643-645

An Accounting Cycle for a Corporation: Journalizing and Posting Transactions

1.

GENERAL JOURNAL   PAGE 12

	DATE	ACCOUNT TITLE	DOC. NO.	POST. REF.	DEBIT	CREDIT	
1	20X4 Dec. 6	Supplies	M25	1140	7 2 4 80		1
2		Accounts Payable/Dreyfus Company		2105/220		7 2 4 80	2
3	7	Notes Receivable	NR30	1125	7 2 0 0 00		3
4		Accounts Receivable/Northside Catering		1115/150		7 2 0 0 00	4
5	9	Allowance for Uncollectible Accounts	M26	1120	4 9 2 0 00		5
6		Accounts Receivable/Ferndale Café		1115/120		4 9 2 0 00	6
7	14	Depreciation Expense—Warehouse Equipment	M27	6125	8 8 0 00		7
8		Accum. Depreciation—Warehouse Equipment		1220		8 8 0 00	8
9	14	Accounts Payable/Glommen Company	DM20	2105/230	3 9 6 00		9
10		Purchases Returns and Allowances		5115		3 9 6 00	10
11	15	Payroll Taxes Expense	M28	6140	5 0 0 90		11
12		Social Security Tax Payable		2135		3 4 9 68	12
13		Medicare Tax Payable		2140		8 1 78	13
14		Unemployment Tax Payable—State		2150		6 0 48	14
15		Unemployment Tax Payable—Federal		2155		8 96	15
16	22	Sales Returns and Allowances	CM8	4115	2 4 0 00		16
17		Sales Tax Payable		2110	1 4 40		17
18		Accounts Receivable/Rao Deli		1115/160		2 5 4 40	18
19							19
20							20
21							21
22							22
23							23
24							24
25							25
26							26
27							27
28							28
29							29
30							30
31							31
32							32

SALES JOURNAL   PAGE 12

	DATE		ACCOUNT DEBITED	SALE NO.	POST. REF.	ACCOUNTS RECEIVABLE DEBIT (1)	SALES CREDIT (2)	SALES TAX PAYABLE CREDIT (3)	
1	20X4 Dec.	5	Huang Restaurant	425	140	1 0 6 0 00	1 0 0 0 00	6 0 00	1
2		9	Rao Deli	426	160	1 0 1 7 60	9 6 0 00	5 7 60	2
3		20	Hilltop Hospital	427	130	3 1 2 0 00	3 1 2 0 00		3
4									4
5									5
6									6
7									7
8									8
9									9
10									10
11									11
12									12
13									13
14									14
15									15
16									16
17									17
18									18
19									19
20									20
21									21
22									22
23									23
24									24
25									25
26									26
27									27
28									28
29									29
30									30
31									31
32									32

REINFORCEMENT ACTIVITY 3, Part A (continued)

1., 3.

PURCHASES JOURNAL

PAGE 12

	DATE		ACCOUNT CREDITED	PURCH. NO.	POST. REF.	PURCHASES DR. ACCTS. PAY. CR.	
1	20X4 Dec.	8	Glommen Company	187	230	9 0 3 6 00	1
2		12	Hilton Supply	188	240	13 6 2 4 00	2
3		16	Bok Supply Company	189	210	9 6 6 6 00	3
4							4
5							5
6							6
7							7
8							8
9							9
10							10
11							11
12							12
13							13
14							14
15							15
16							16
17							17
18							18
19							19
20							20
21							21
22							22
23							23
24							24
25							25
26							26
27							27
28							28
29							29
30							30
31							31
32							32

PAGE 12

1., 4., 6.

CASH RECEIPTS JOURNAL

DATE		ACCOUNT TITLE	DOC. NO.	POST. REF.	GENERAL DEBIT	GENERAL CREDIT	ACCOUNTS RECEIVABLE CREDIT	SALES CREDIT	SALES TAX PAYABLE CREDIT	SALES DISCOUNT DEBIT	CASH DEBIT	
20X4 Dec.	2	Rao Deli	R451	160			6 5 0 0 00				6 5 0 0 00	1
	6		TS37	✔				10 8 6 0 00	6 5 1 60		11 5 1 1 60	2
	12	Huang Restaurant	R452	140			1 0 6 0 00			2 1 20	1 0 3 8 80	3
	13		TS38	✔				11 9 7 4 00	7 1 8 44		12 6 9 2 44	4
	14	Accum. Depr.—Warehouse Equip.	R453	1220	3 7 6 0 00						2 8 0 0 00	5
		Warehouse Equipment		1215		5 8 0 0 00						6
		Gain on Plant Assets		7115		7 6 00						7
	20		TS39	✔				7 1 0 8 00	4 2 6 48		7 5 3 4 48	8
												9
												10
												11
												12
												13
												14
												15
												16
												17
												18
												19
												20
												21
												22
												23
												24
												25

REINFORCEMENT ACTIVITY 3, Part A (continued)

5.

Cash on hand at the beginning of the month . . . .   _____

    Plus total cash received during the month . . . .   _____

    Equals total . . . .   _____

    Less total cash paid during the month . . . .   _____

    Equals cash balance on hand at the end of the month . . . .   _____

Checkbook balance on the next unused check stub . . . .   _____

1., 4., 7.

CASH PAYMENTS JOURNAL

PAGE 23

	DATE		ACCOUNT TITLE	CK. NO.	POST. REF.	GENERAL DEBIT	GENERAL CREDIT	ACCOUNTS PAYABLE DEBIT	PURCHASES DISCOUNT CREDIT	CASH CREDIT	
1	20X4 Dec.	1	Rent Expense	331	6145	3 5 0 0 00				3 5 0 0 00	1
2		3	Winona Manufacturing	332	260			1 2 4 0 00	2 4 80	1 2 1 5 20	2
3		3	Notes Payable	333	2115	20 0 0 0 00				20 9 0 0 00	3
4			Interest Expense		8105	9 0 0 00					4
5		5	Office Equipment	334	1205	2 4 0 0 00				2 4 0 0 00	5
6		10	Supplies	335	1140	4 4 6 00				4 4 6 00	6
7		15	Employee Income Tax Payable	336	2130	6 4 8 00				2 4 5 6 70	7
8			Social Security Tax Payable		2135	1 4 8 4 00					8
9			Medicare Tax Payable		2140	3 2 4 70					9
10		15	Salary Expense	337	6155	5 6 4 0 00				4 5 1 2 54	10
11			Employee Income Tax Payable		2130		3 1 6 00				11
12			Social Security Tax Payable		2135		3 4 9 68				12
13			Medicare Tax Payable		2140		8 1 78				13
14			Medical Insurance Payable		2145		3 8 0 00				14
15		17	Utilities Expense	338	6170	6 9 2 40				6 9 2 40	15
16		17	Glommen Company	339	230			9 0 3 6 00	1 8 0 72	8 8 5 5 28	16
17		19	Miscellaneous Expense	340	6135	1 4 4 00				1 4 4 00	17
18		21	Purchases	341	5105	7 1 4 00				7 1 4 00	18
19		23	Hilton Supply	342	240			13 6 2 4 00		13 6 2 4 00	19
20											20
21											21
22											22
23											23
24											24
25											25
26											26
27											27
28											28
29											29
30											30
31											31
32											32
33											33
34											34
35											35

REINFORCEMENT ACTIVITY 3, Part A (continued)

1., 9.

PLANT ASSET RECORD No. __215__   General Ledger Account No. __1215__

Description __Lift Cart__   General Ledger Account __Warehouse Equipment__

Date Bought __January 5, 20X1__   Serial Number __65-B458__   Original Cost __$5,800.00__

Estimated Useful Life __5 years__   Estimated Salvage Value __$1,000.00__   Depreciation Method __Straight-line__

Disposed of: Discarded _____   Sold ✔ _____   Traded _____

Date __December 14, 20X4__   Disposal Amount __$2,800.00__

Year	Annual Depreciation Expense	Accumulated Depreciation	Ending Book Value
20X1	$960.00	$ 960.00	$4,840.00
20X2	960.00	1,920.00	3,880.00
20X3	960.00	2,880.00	2,920.00
20X4	880.00	3,760.00	2,040.00

PLANT ASSET RECORD No. __284__   General Ledger Account No. __1205__

Description __Computer__   General Ledger Account __Office Equipment__

Date Bought __April 5, 20X2__   Serial Number __3545723Y5D85Z__   Original Cost __$1,700.00__

Estimated Useful Life __3 years__   Estimated Salvage Value __$260.00__   Depreciation Method __Straight-line__

Disposed of: Discarded _____   Sold ✔ _____   Traded _____

Date _____   Disposal Amount _____

Year	Annual Depreciation Expense	Accumulated Depreciation	Ending Book Value
20X2	$360.00	$ 360.00	$1,340.00
20X3	480.00	840.00	860.00

9.

PLANT ASSET RECORD No. 422		General Ledger Account No. 1205
Description Fax Machine		General Ledger Account Office Equipment

Date Bought December 5, 20X4 Serial Number BG-342XG Original Cost $2,400.00

Estimated Useful Life 3 years Estimated Salvage Value $400.00 Depreciation Method Straight-line

Disposed of: _____ Discarded _____ Sold _____ Traded _____

Date _____ Disposal Amount _____

Year	Annual Depreciation Expense	Accumulated Depreciation	Ending Book Value

PLANT ASSET RECORD No. _____		General Ledger Account No. _____
Description _____		General Ledger Account _____

Date Bought _____ Serial Number _____ Original Cost _____

Estimated Useful Life _____ Estimated Salvage Value _____ Depreciation Method _____

Disposed of: _____ Discarded _____ Sold _____ Traded _____

Date _____ Disposal Amount _____

Year	Annual Depreciation Expense	Accumulated Depreciation	Ending Book Value

REINFORCEMENT ACTIVITY 3, Part A (continued)

PLANT ASSET RECORD No. _____   General Ledger Account No. _____

Description _____   General Ledger Account _____

Date Bought _____   Serial Number _____   Original Cost _____

Estimated Useful Life _____   Estimated Salvage Value _____   Depreciation Method _____

Disposed of: Discarded _____   Sold _____   Traded _____

Date _____   Disposal Amount _____

Year	Annual Depreciation Expense	Accumulated Depreciation	Ending Book Value

REINFORCEMENT ACTIVITY 3, Part A (continued)

1.   ACCOUNTS RECEIVABLE LEDGER

ACCOUNT Bakery Depot   ACCOUNT NO. 110

DATE	ITEM	POST. REF.	DEBIT	CREDIT	DEBIT BALANCE

ACCOUNT Ferndale Café   ACCOUNT NO. 120

DATE		ITEM	POST. REF.	DEBIT	CREDIT	DEBIT BALANCE
20X4 Dec.	1	Balance	✔			4 9 2 0 00
	9	Written Off	G12		4 9 2 0 00	—

ACCOUNT Hilltop Hospital   ACCOUNT NO. 130

DATE		ITEM	POST. REF.	DEBIT	CREDIT	DEBIT BALANCE
20X4 Dec.	1	Balance	✔			4 8 6 00
	20		S12	3 1 2 0 00		3 6 0 6 00

ACCOUNT Huang Restaurant   ACCOUNT NO. 140

DATE		ITEM	POST. REF.	DEBIT	CREDIT	DEBIT BALANCE
20X4 Dec.	5		S12	1 0 6 0 00		1 0 6 0 00
	12		CR12		1 0 6 0 00	—

REINFORCEMENT ACTIVITY 3, Part A (continued)

ACCOUNT Northside Catering   ACCOUNT NO. 150

DATE		ITEM	POST. REF.	DEBIT	CREDIT	DEBIT BALANCE
20X4 Dec.	1	Balance	✔			7 2 0 0 00
	7	Accepted note receivable	G12		7 2 0 0 00	————

ACCOUNT Rao Deli   ACCOUNT NO. 160

DATE		ITEM	POST. REF.	DEBIT	CREDIT	DEBIT BALANCE
20X4 Dec.	1	Balance	✔			6 5 0 0 00
	2		CR12		6 5 0 0 00	————
	9		S12	1 0 1 7 60		1 0 1 7 60
	22		G12		2 5 4 40	7 6 3 20

8.

1.   **ACCOUNTS PAYABLE LEDGER**

ACCOUNT Bok Supply Company   ACCOUNT NO. 210

DATE		ITEM	POST. REF.	DEBIT	CREDIT	CREDIT BALANCE
20X4 Dec.	1	Balance	✔			2 5 4 4 00
	16		P12		9 6 6 6 00	12 2 1 0 00

ACCOUNT Dreyfus Company   ACCOUNT NO. 220

DATE		ITEM	POST. REF.	DEBIT	CREDIT	CREDIT BALANCE
20X4 Dec.	1	Balance	✔			2 8 3 4 50
	6		G12		7 2 4 80	3 5 5 9 30

ACCOUNT Glommen Company   ACCOUNT NO. 230

DATE		ITEM	POST. REF.	DEBIT	CREDIT	CREDIT BALANCE
20X4 Dec.	1	Balance	✔			3 9 6 00
	8		P12		9 0 3 6 00	9 4 3 2 00
	14		G12	3 9 6 00		9 0 3 6 00
	17		CP23	9 0 3 6 00		—

ACCOUNT Hilton Supply   ACCOUNT NO. 240

DATE		ITEM	POST. REF.	DEBIT	CREDIT	CREDIT BALANCE
20X4 Dec.	12		P12		13 6 2 4 00	13 6 2 4 00
	23		CP23	13 6 2 4 00		—

ACCOUNT **Sarr Corp.**   ACCOUNT NO. 250

DATE		ITEM	POST. REF.	DEBIT	CREDIT	CREDIT BALANCE
20X4 Dec.	1	Balance	✔			1 1 6 0 00

ACCOUNT **Winona Manufacturing**   ACCOUNT NO. 260

DATE		ITEM	POST. REF.	DEBIT	CREDIT	CREDIT BALANCE
20X4 Dec.	1	Balance	✔			1 2 4 0 00
	3		CP23	1 2 4 0 00		—

8.

1., 2., 3., 6., 7., 11., 12., 15., 21., 23.

GENERAL LEDGER

ACCOUNT Cash   ACCOUNT NO. 1105

DATE		ITEM	POST. REF.	DEBIT	CREDIT	BALANCE DEBIT	BALANCE CREDIT
20X4 Dec.	1	Balance	✔			7 9 1 9 60	

ACCOUNT Petty Cash   ACCOUNT NO. 1110

DATE		ITEM	POST. REF.	DEBIT	CREDIT	BALANCE DEBIT	BALANCE CREDIT
20X4 Dec.	1	Balance	✔			4 0 0 00	

ACCOUNT Accounts Receivable   ACCOUNT NO. 1115

DATE		ITEM	POST. REF.	DEBIT	CREDIT	BALANCE DEBIT	BALANCE CREDIT
20X4 Dec.	1	Balance	✔			19 1 0 6 00	
	7		G12		7 2 0 0 00	11 9 0 6 00	
	9		G12		4 9 2 0 00	6 9 8 6 00	
	22		G12		2 5 4 40	6 7 3 1 60	

REINFORCEMENT ACTIVITY 3, Part A (continued)

ACCOUNT Allowance for Uncollectible Accounts   ACCOUNT NO. 1120

DATE		ITEM	POST. REF.	DEBIT	CREDIT	BALANCE DEBIT	BALANCE CREDIT
20X4 Dec.	1	Balance	✔				8 5 20
	9		G12	4 9 2 0 00		4 8 3 4 80	

ACCOUNT Notes Receivable   ACCOUNT NO. 1125

DATE		ITEM	POST. REF.	DEBIT	CREDIT	BALANCE DEBIT	BALANCE CREDIT
20X4 Dec.	1	Balance	✔			17 6 0 0 00	
	7		G12	7 2 0 0 00		24 8 0 0 00	

ACCOUNT Interest Receivable   ACCOUNT NO. 1130

DATE		ITEM	POST. REF.	DEBIT	CREDIT	BALANCE DEBIT	BALANCE CREDIT

ACCOUNT Merchandise Inventory   ACCOUNT NO. 1135

DATE		ITEM	POST. REF.	DEBIT	CREDIT	BALANCE DEBIT	BALANCE CREDIT
20X4 Dec.	1	Balance	✔			148 3 5 3 90	

ACCOUNT Supplies   ACCOUNT NO. 1140

DATE		ITEM	POST. REF.	DEBIT	CREDIT	BALANCE DEBIT	BALANCE CREDIT
20X4 Dec.	1	Balance	✔			5 0 0 2 30	
	6		G12	7 2 4 80		5 7 2 7 10	
	10		CP23	4 4 6 00		6 1 7 3 10	

ACCOUNT Prepaid Insurance   ACCOUNT NO. 1145

DATE		ITEM	POST. REF.	DEBIT	CREDIT	BALANCE DEBIT	BALANCE CREDIT
20X4 Dec.	1	Balance	✔			17 2 0 0 00	

REINFORCEMENT ACTIVITY 3, Part A (continued)

ACCOUNT Office Equipment   ACCOUNT NO. 1205

DATE		ITEM	POST. REF.	DEBIT	CREDIT	BALANCE DEBIT	BALANCE CREDIT
20X4 Dec.	1	Balance	✔			66 9 6 0 00	
	5		CP23	2 4 0 0 00		69 3 6 0 00	

ACCOUNT Accumulated Depreciation—Office Equipment   ACCOUNT NO. 1210

DATE		ITEM	POST. REF.	DEBIT	CREDIT	BALANCE DEBIT	BALANCE CREDIT
20X4 Dec.	1	Balance	✔				15 1 6 0 00

ACCOUNT Warehouse Equipment   ACCOUNT NO. 1215

DATE		ITEM	POST. REF.	DEBIT	CREDIT	BALANCE DEBIT	BALANCE CREDIT
20X4 Dec.	1	Balance	✔			78 0 2 0 00	
	14		CR12		5 8 0 0 00	72 2 2 0 00	

ACCOUNT Accumulated Depreciation—Warehouse Equipment   ACCOUNT NO. 1220

DATE		ITEM	POST. REF.	DEBIT	CREDIT	BALANCE DEBIT	BALANCE CREDIT
20X4 Dec.	1	Balance	✔				16 960 00
	14		G12		880 00		17 840 00
	14		CR12	3 760 00			14 080 00

ACCOUNT Accounts Payable   ACCOUNT NO. 2105

DATE		ITEM	POST. REF.	DEBIT	CREDIT	BALANCE DEBIT	BALANCE CREDIT
20X4 Dec.	1	Balance	✔				8 174 50
	6		G12		724 80		8 899 30
	14		G12	396 00			8 503 30

ACCOUNT Sales Tax Payable   ACCOUNT NO. 2110

DATE		ITEM	POST. REF.	DEBIT	CREDIT	BALANCE DEBIT	BALANCE CREDIT
20X4 Dec.	1	Balance	✔				9 885 36
	22		G12	14 40			9 870 96

REINFORCEMENT ACTIVITY 3, Part A (continued)

ACCOUNT Notes Payable   ACCOUNT NO. 2115

DATE		ITEM	POST. REF.	DEBIT	CREDIT	BALANCE DEBIT	BALANCE CREDIT
20X4 Dec.	1	Balance	✔				40 0 0 0 00
	3		CP23	20 0 0 0 00			20 0 0 0 00

ACCOUNT Interest Payable   ACCOUNT NO. 2120

DATE	ITEM	POST. REF.	DEBIT	CREDIT	BALANCE DEBIT	BALANCE CREDIT

ACCOUNT Unearned Rent Income   ACCOUNT NO. 2125

DATE		ITEM	POST. REF.	DEBIT	CREDIT	BALANCE DEBIT	BALANCE CREDIT
20X4 Dec.	1	Balance	✔				10 0 0 0 00

ACCOUNT Employee Income Tax Payable   ACCOUNT NO. 2130

DATE		ITEM	POST. REF.	DEBIT	CREDIT	BALANCE DEBIT	BALANCE CREDIT
20X4 Dec.	1	Balance	✔				6 4 8 00
	15		CP23	6 4 8 00			—
	15		CP23		3 1 6 00		3 1 6 00

ACCOUNT Social Security Tax Payable   ACCOUNT NO. 2135

DATE		ITEM	POST. REF.	DEBIT	CREDIT	BALANCE DEBIT	BALANCE CREDIT
20X4 Dec.	1	Balance	✔				1 4 8 4 00
	15		G12		3 4 9 68		1 8 3 3 68
	15		CP23	1 4 8 4 00			3 4 9 68
	15		CP23		3 4 9 68		6 9 9 36

ACCOUNT Medicare Tax Payable   ACCOUNT NO. 2140

DATE		ITEM	POST. REF.	DEBIT	CREDIT	BALANCE DEBIT	BALANCE CREDIT
20X4 Dec.	1	Balance	✔				3 2 4 70
	15		G12		8 1 78		4 0 6 48
	15		CP23	3 2 4 70			8 1 78
	15		CP23		8 1 78		1 6 3 56

REINFORCEMENT ACTIVITY 3, Part A (continued)

ACCOUNT Medical Insurance Payable   ACCOUNT NO. 2145

DATE		ITEM	POST. REF.	DEBIT	CREDIT	BALANCE	
						DEBIT	CREDIT
Dec.	1	Balance	✔				1 4 5 0 00
	15		CP23		3 8 0 00		1 8 3 0 00

ACCOUNT Unemployment Tax Payable—State   ACCOUNT NO. 2150

DATE		ITEM	POST. REF.	DEBIT	CREDIT	BALANCE	
						DEBIT	CREDIT
Dec.	1	Balance	✔				1 7 6 10
	15		G12		6 0 48		2 3 6 58

ACCOUNT Unemployment Tax Payable—Federal   ACCOUNT NO. 2155

DATE		ITEM	POST. REF.	DEBIT	CREDIT	BALANCE	
						DEBIT	CREDIT
Dec.	1	Balance	✔				2 6 10
	15		G12		8 96		3 5 06

ACCOUNT Federal Income Tax Payable — ACCOUNT NO. 2160

DATE	ITEM	POST. REF.	DEBIT	CREDIT	BALANCE DEBIT	BALANCE CREDIT

ACCOUNT Dividends Payable — ACCOUNT NO. 2165

DATE	ITEM	POST. REF.	DEBIT	CREDIT	BALANCE DEBIT	BALANCE CREDIT
20X4 Dec. 1	Balance	✔				10 000 00

ACCOUNT Bonds Payable — ACCOUNT NO. 2205

DATE	ITEM	POST. REF.	DEBIT	CREDIT	BALANCE DEBIT	BALANCE CREDIT
20X4 Dec. 1	Balance	✔				30 000 00

REINFORCEMENT ACTIVITY 3, Part A (continued)

ACCOUNT Capital Stock—Common   ACCOUNT NO. 3105

DATE	ITEM	POST. REF.	DEBIT	CREDIT	BALANCE DEBIT	BALANCE CREDIT
20X4 Dec. 1	Balance	✔				60 0 0 0 00

ACCOUNT Paid-in Capital in Excess of Par—Common   ACCOUNT NO. 3110

DATE	ITEM	POST. REF.	DEBIT	CREDIT	BALANCE DEBIT	BALANCE CREDIT

ACCOUNT Capital Stock—Preferred   ACCOUNT NO. 3115

DATE	ITEM	POST. REF.	DEBIT	CREDIT	BALANCE DEBIT	BALANCE CREDIT

ACCOUNT Paid-in Capital in Excess of Par—Preferred

ACCOUNT NO. 3120

DATE		ITEM	POST. REF.	DEBIT	CREDIT	BALANCE	
						DEBIT	CREDIT

ACCOUNT Retained Earnings

ACCOUNT NO. 3205

DATE		ITEM	POST. REF.	DEBIT	CREDIT	BALANCE	
						DEBIT	CREDIT
20X4 Dec.	1	Balance	✔				47 7 7 8 40

ACCOUNT Dividends

ACCOUNT NO. 3210

DATE		ITEM	POST. REF.	DEBIT	CREDIT	BALANCE	
						DEBIT	CREDIT
20X4 Dec.	1	Balance	✔			40 0 0 0 00	

REINFORCEMENT ACTIVITY 3, Part A (continued)

ACCOUNT Income Summary   ACCOUNT NO. 3215

DATE	ITEM	POST. REF.	DEBIT	CREDIT	BALANCE DEBIT	BALANCE CREDIT

ACCOUNT Sales   ACCOUNT NO. 4105

DATE	ITEM	POST. REF.	DEBIT	CREDIT	BALANCE DEBIT	BALANCE CREDIT
20X4 Dec. 1	Balance	✔				1512 7 9 5 80

ACCOUNT Sales Discount   ACCOUNT NO. 4110

DATE	ITEM	POST. REF.	DEBIT	CREDIT	BALANCE DEBIT	BALANCE CREDIT
20X4 Dec. 1	Balance	✔			3 7 5 7 20	

ACCOUNT **Sales Returns and Allowances** ACCOUNT NO. 4115

DATE		ITEM	POST. REF.	DEBIT	CREDIT	BALANCE DEBIT	BALANCE CREDIT
20X4 Dec.	1	Balance	✔			12 1 0 9 60	
	22		G12	2 4 0 00		12 3 4 9 60	

ACCOUNT **Purchases** ACCOUNT NO. 5105

DATE		ITEM	POST. REF.	DEBIT	CREDIT	BALANCE DEBIT	BALANCE CREDIT
20X4 Dec.	1	Balance	✔			1012 7 0 8 80	
	21		CP23	7 1 4 00		1013 4 2 2 80	

ACCOUNT **Purchases Discount** ACCOUNT NO. 5110

DATE		ITEM	POST. REF.	DEBIT	CREDIT	BALANCE DEBIT	BALANCE CREDIT
20X4 Dec.	1	Balance	✔				6 9 8 6 64

REINFORCEMENT ACTIVITY 3, Part A (continued)

ACCOUNT Purchases Returns and Allowances   ACCOUNT NO. 5115

DATE		ITEM	POST. REF.	DEBIT	CREDIT	BALANCE DEBIT	BALANCE CREDIT
20X4 Dec.	1	Balance	✔				6 0 7 6 00
	14		G12		3 9 6 00		6 4 7 2 00

ACCOUNT Advertising Expense   ACCOUNT NO. 6105

DATE		ITEM	POST. REF.	DEBIT	CREDIT	BALANCE DEBIT	BALANCE CREDIT
20X4 Dec.	1	Balance	✔			19 1 1 3 40	

ACCOUNT Cash Short and Over   ACCOUNT NO. 6110

DATE		ITEM	POST. REF.	DEBIT	CREDIT	BALANCE DEBIT	BALANCE CREDIT
20X4 Dec.	1	Balance	✔			4 0 00	

ACCOUNT Credit Card Fee Expense   ACCOUNT NO. 6115

DATE		ITEM	POST. REF.	DEBIT	CREDIT	BALANCE DEBIT	BALANCE CREDIT
20X4 Dec.	1	Balance	✔			28 2 2 2 80	

ACCOUNT Depreciation Expense—Office Equipment   ACCOUNT NO. 6120

DATE		ITEM	POST. REF.	DEBIT	CREDIT	BALANCE DEBIT	BALANCE CREDIT

ACCOUNT Depreciation Expense—Warehouse Equipment   ACCOUNT NO. 6125

DATE		ITEM	POST. REF.	DEBIT	CREDIT	BALANCE DEBIT	BALANCE CREDIT
20X4 Dec.	14		G12	8 8 0 00		8 8 0 00	

REINFORCEMENT ACTIVITY 3, Part A (continued)

ACCOUNT Insurance Expense   ACCOUNT NO. 6130

DATE	ITEM	POST. REF.	DEBIT	CREDIT	BALANCE DEBIT	BALANCE CREDIT

ACCOUNT Miscellaneous Expense   ACCOUNT NO. 6135

DATE	ITEM	POST. REF.	DEBIT	CREDIT	BALANCE DEBIT	BALANCE CREDIT
20X4 Dec. 1	Balance	✔			11 4 6 7 90	
19		CP23	1 4 4 00		11 6 1 1 90	

ACCOUNT Payroll Taxes Expense   ACCOUNT NO. 6140

DATE	ITEM	POST. REF.	DEBIT	CREDIT	BALANCE DEBIT	BALANCE CREDIT
20X4 Dec. 1	Balance	✔			20 3 5 3 70	
15		G12	5 0 0 90		20 8 5 4 60	

REINFORCEMENT ACTIVITY 3, Part A (continued)

ACCOUNT Rent Expense   ACCOUNT NO. 6145

DATE		ITEM	POST. REF.	DEBIT	CREDIT	BALANCE DEBIT	BALANCE CREDIT
20X4 Dec.	1	Balance	✔			38 500 00	
	1		CP23	3 500 00		42 000 00	

ACCOUNT Repairs Expense   ACCOUNT NO. 6150

DATE		ITEM	POST. REF.	DEBIT	CREDIT	BALANCE DEBIT	BALANCE CREDIT
20X4 Dec.	1	Balance	✔			2 789 60	

ACCOUNT Salary Expense   ACCOUNT NO. 6155

DATE		ITEM	POST. REF.	DEBIT	CREDIT	BALANCE DEBIT	BALANCE CREDIT
20X4 Dec.	1	Balance	✔			198 596 00	
	15		CP23	5 640 00		204 236 00	

REINFORCEMENT ACTIVITY 3, Part A (continued)

ACCOUNT Supplies Expense   ACCOUNT NO. 6160

DATE	ITEM	POST. REF.	DEBIT	CREDIT	BALANCE DEBIT	BALANCE CREDIT

ACCOUNT Uncollectible Accounts Expense   ACCOUNT NO. 6165

DATE	ITEM	POST. REF.	DEBIT	CREDIT	BALANCE DEBIT	BALANCE CREDIT

ACCOUNT Utilities Expense   ACCOUNT NO. 6170

DATE	ITEM	POST. REF.	DEBIT	CREDIT	BALANCE DEBIT	BALANCE CREDIT
20X4 Dec. 1	Balance	✔			13 7 8 0 00	
17		CP23	6 9 2 40		14 4 7 2 40	

REINFORCEMENT ACTIVITY 3, Part A (continued)

ACCOUNT Federal Income Tax Expense   ACCOUNT NO. 6205

DATE		ITEM	POST. REF.	DEBIT	CREDIT	BALANCE DEBIT	BALANCE CREDIT
20X4 Dec.	1	Balance	✔			12 000 00	

ACCOUNT Interest Income   ACCOUNT NO. 7105

DATE		ITEM	POST. REF.	DEBIT	CREDIT	BALANCE DEBIT	BALANCE CREDIT
20X4 Dec.	1	Balance	✔				360 00

ACCOUNT Rent Income   ACCOUNT NO. 7110

DATE		ITEM	POST. REF.	DEBIT	CREDIT	BALANCE DEBIT	BALANCE CREDIT

REINFORCEMENT ACTIVITY 3, Part A (concluded)

ACCOUNT Gain on Plant Assets   ACCOUNT NO. 7115

DATE		ITEM	POST. REF.	DEBIT	CREDIT	BALANCE DEBIT	BALANCE CREDIT
20X4 Dec.	1	Balance	✔				7 3 0 00
	14		CR12		7 6 0 00		1 4 9 0 00

ACCOUNT Interest Expense   ACCOUNT NO. 8105

DATE		ITEM	POST. REF.	DEBIT	CREDIT	BALANCE DEBIT	BALANCE CREDIT
20X4 Dec.	1	Balance	✔			4 6 0 0 00	
	3		CP23	9 0 0 00		5 5 0 0 00	

ACCOUNT Loss on Plant Assets   ACCOUNT NO. 8110

DATE		ITEM	POST. REF.	DEBIT	CREDIT	BALANCE DEBIT	BALANCE CREDIT
20X4 Dec.	1	Balance	✔			5 0 0 00	

Study Guide 21

Name		Perfect Score	Your Score
	Identifying Accounting Terms	7 Pts.	
	Analyzing Accounts Affected by Accruals and Deferrals	30 Pts.	
	Analyzing Accruals and Deferrals	13 Pts.	
	Total	50 Pts.	

Part One—Identifying Accounting Terms

Directions: Select the one term in Column I that best fits each definition in Column II. Print the letter identifying your choice in the Answers column.

Column I	Column II	Answers
A. accrual	1. An entry recording revenue before the cash is received or an expense before the cash is paid. (p. 648)	1. _____
B. accrued interest expense	2. An entry recording the receipt of cash before the related revenue is earned or payment of cash before the related expense is incurred. (p. 648)	2. _____
C. accrued expenses	3. An entry made at the beginning of one fiscal period to reverse an adjusting entry made in a previous fiscal period. (p. 649)	3. _____
D. deferral	4. Expenses incurred in one fiscal period but not paid until a later fiscal period. (p. 652)	4. _____
E. deferred expenses	5. Interest incurred but not yet paid. (p. 652)	5. _____
F. deferred revenue	6. Cash received for goods or services which have not yet been provided. (p. 658)	6. _____
G. reversing entry	7. Payments for goods or services which have not yet been received. (p. 660)	7. _____

Part Two—Analyzing Accounts Affected by Accruals and Deferrals

Directions: Determine in which journal each of the transactions is to be recorded. Analyze each of the following entries into debit and credit parts. Print letters (A through K) in the proper Answers columns identifying the accounts to be debited and credited.

G—General Journal; CP—Cash Payments Journal; CR—Cash Receipts Journal

Account Titles	Transactions	Answers 1 Journal	2 Debit	3 Credit
A. Cash	1–2–3. Recorded an adjustment for accrued interest income. (p. 649)	1. _____	2. _____	3. _____
B. Interest Expense	4–5–6. Reversed an adjusting entry for accrued interest income. (p. 649)	4. _____	5. _____	6. _____
C. Interest Income	7–8–9. Received cash for the maturity value of a 120-day, 10% note. (p. 650)	7. _____	8. _____	9. _____
D. Interest Payable	10–11–12. Recorded an adjustment for accrued interest expense. (p. 652)	10. _____	11. _____	12. _____
E. Interest Receivable	13–14–15. Reversed an adjusting entry for accrued interest expense. (p. 653)	13. _____	14. _____	15. _____
F. Notes Payable	16–17–18. Paid cash for the maturity value of a note payable plus interest. (p. 654)	16. _____	17. _____	18. _____
G. Notes Receivable	19–20–21. Recorded rent revenue received in advance. (p. 658)	19. _____	20. _____	21. _____
H. Prepaid Rent	22–23–24. Recorded adjusting entry for rent income earned which had previously been received. (p. 659)	22. _____	23. _____	24. _____
I. Rent Expense	25–26–27. Recorded rent expense paid in advance. (p. 660)	25. _____	26. _____	27. _____
J. Rent Income	28–29–30. Recorded adjusting entry for rent expense incurred which had previously been paid. (p. 661)	28. _____	29. _____	30. _____
K. Unearned Rent Income				

Part Three—Analyzing Accruals and Deferrals

Directions: Place a T for True or an F for False in the Answers column to show whether each of the following statements is true or false.

Answers

1. Revenue and expenses should be recorded when the revenue is earned and expenses are incurred. (p. 648)

    1. _____

2. Accrued interest income is credited to the Interest Income account. (p. 649)

    2. _____

3. The reversing entry for accrued interest earned includes a credit to the Interest Income account. (p. 649)

    3. _____

4. Recording an adjusting entry for an accrued expense is an application of the Realization of Revenue concept. (p. 652)

    4. _____

5. At the end of a fiscal period, the Interest Expense balance after adjustments shows the amount of interest expense that has been incurred in that fiscal period. (p. 653)

    5. _____

6. When a reversing entry is made for accrued interest expense, a credit entry to Interest Payable is required. (p. 653)

    6. _____

7. Reversing entries are not required in accounting. (p. 654)

    7. _____

8. If cash is received for revenue that has not been earned, a liability is increased. (p. 658)

    8. _____

9. The adjusting entry for deferred rent revenue earned increases the Unearned Rent Income account. (p. 659)

    9. _____

10. The adjusting entry for deferred rent revenue earned includes a credit to Rent Income. (p. 659)

    10. _____

11. If cash is paid for a deferred expense, an asset is increased. (p. 660)

    11. _____

12. The adjusting entry for deferred rent expense increases the Rent Expense account. (p. 661)

    12. _____

13. The adjusting entry for deferred rent expense incurred includes a credit to Prepaid Rent. (p. 661)

    13. _____

Across

2. An entry recording revenue before the cash is received, or an expense before the cash is paid.

5. An entry recording the receipt of cash before the related revenue is earned, or payment of cash before the related expense is incurred.

6. An entry made at the beginning of one fiscal period to reverse an adjusting entry made in the previous fiscal period.

7. Anything, or any process, that is protected by patent, trademark, or copyright.

Down

1. Payments for goods or services which have not yet been received.

3. Expenses incurred in one fiscal period, but not paid until a later fiscal period.

4. Cash received for goods or services which have not yet been provided.

21-1 WORK TOGETHER, p. 656

Journalizing entries for accruals

Kufas Corporation
Unadjusted Trial Balance
December 31, 20X1

ACCOUNT TITLE	DEBIT	CREDIT
Notes Receivable	10 000 00	
Interest Receivable		
Notes Payable		12 000 00
Interest Payable		
Interest Income		3 090 00
Interest Expense	1 315 00	

1., 2.

GENERAL JOURNAL

PAGE ____

	DATE	ACCOUNT TITLE	DOC. NO.	POST. REF.	DEBIT	CREDIT	
1							1
2							2
3							3
4							4
5							5
6							6
7							7
8							8
9							9
10							10
11							11

3.

GENERAL JOURNAL

PAGE ____

	DATE	ACCOUNT TITLE	DOC. NO.	POST. REF.	DEBIT	CREDIT	
1							1
2							2
3							3
4							4
5							5

4.

CASH PAYMENTS JOURNAL

PAGE 5

				1 GENERAL		3 ACCOUNTS PAYABLE DEBIT	4 PURCHASES DISCOUNT CREDIT	5 CASH CREDIT	
DATE	ACCOUNT TITLE	CK. NO.	POST. REF.	1 DEBIT	2 CREDIT				
									1
									2
									3
									4
									5
									6

5.

CASH RECEIPTS JOURNAL

PAGE 7

				1 GENERAL		3 ACCOUNTS RECEIVABLE CREDIT	4 SALES CREDIT	5 SALES TAX PAYABLE CREDIT	6 SALES DISCOUNT DEBIT	7 CASH DEBIT	
DATE	ACCOUNT TITLE	DOC. NO.	POST. REF.	1 DEBIT	2 CREDIT						
											1
											2
											3
											4
											5
											6

21-1 WORK TOGETHER (concluded)

1., 2., 3., 4., 5.

Notes Receivable			Notes Payable	
Nov. 16	10,000.00		Dec. 1	12,000.00

Interest Receivable		Interest Payable	

Income Summary		Interest Income	
		Dec. 31 Bal.	3,090.00

Interest Expense	
Dec. 31 Bal.	1,315.00

6. Interest Income for 20X1 _____
Interest Income for 20X2 _____

7. Interest Expense for 20X1 _____
Interest Expense for 20X2 _____

Journalizing entries for accruals

Craven, Inc.

Unadjusted Trial Balance

December 31, 20X1

ACCOUNT TITLE	DEBIT	CREDIT
Notes Receivable	12 0 0 0 00	
Interest Receivable		
Notes Payable		20 0 0 0 00
Interest Payable		
Interest Income		2 3 2 1 00
Interest Expense	1 6 2 1 00	

1., 2.

GENERAL JOURNAL   PAGE

	DATE	ACCOUNT TITLE	DOC. NO.	POST. REF.	DEBIT	CREDIT	
1							1
2							2
3							3
4							4
5							5
6							6
7							7
8							8
9							9
10							10
11							11

3.

GENERAL JOURNAL   PAGE

	DATE	ACCOUNT TITLE	DOC. NO.	POST. REF.	DEBIT	CREDIT	
1							1
2							2
3							3
4							4
5							5

21-1 **ON YOUR OWN (continued)**

4.

CASH RECEIPTS JOURNAL

PAGE 7

DATE	ACCOUNT TITLE	DOC. NO.	POST. REF.	GENERAL 1 DEBIT	GENERAL 2 CREDIT	ACCOUNTS RECEIVABLE 3 CREDIT	SALES 4 CREDIT	SALES TAX PAYABLE 5 CREDIT	SALES DISCOUNT 6 DEBIT	CASH 7 DEBIT
										1
										2
										3
										4
										5
										6

5.

CASH PAYMENTS JOURNAL

PAGE 5

DATE	ACCOUNT TITLE	CK. NO.	POST. REF.	GENERAL 1 DEBIT	GENERAL 2 CREDIT	ACCOUNTS PAYABLE 3 DEBIT	PURCHASES DISCOUNT 4 CREDIT	CASH 5 CREDIT
								1
								2
								3
								4
								5
								6

Chapter 21 Accounting for Accruals, Deferrals, and Reversing Entries • **125**

1., 2., 3., 4., 5.

Notes Receivable		
Dec. 1	12,000.00	

Notes Payable		
	Oct. 17	20,000.00

Interest Receivable		

Interest Payable		

Income Summary		

Interest Income		
	Dec. 31 Bal.	2,321.00

Interest Expense		
Dec. 31 Bal.	1,621.00	

6. Interest Income for 20X1 _____
Interest Income for 20X2 _____

7. Interest Expense for 20X1 _____
Interest Expense for 20X2 _____

21-2 WORK TOGETHER, p. 663

Journalizing entries for deferrals

1.

CASH RECEIPTS JOURNAL

PAGE 17

				1	2	3	4	5	6	7
				GENERAL		ACCOUNTS RECEIVABLE CREDIT	SALES CREDIT	SALES TAX PAYABLE CREDIT	SALES DISCOUNT DEBIT	CASH DEBIT
DATE	ACCOUNT TITLE	DOC. NO.	POST. REF.	DEBIT	CREDIT					

GENERAL JOURNAL

PAGE 13

DATE	ACCOUNT TITLE	DOC. NO.	POST. REF.	DEBIT	CREDIT

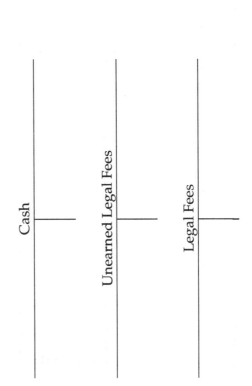

Cash

Unearned Legal Fees

Legal Fees

2.

CASH PAYMENTS JOURNAL

PAGE 17

				1	2	3	4	5
				GENERAL		ACCOUNTS PAYABLE DEBIT	PURCHASES DISCOUNT CREDIT	CASH CREDIT
DATE	ACCOUNT TITLE	CK. NO.	POST. REF.	DEBIT	CREDIT			

GENERAL JOURNAL

PAGE 13

DATE	ACCOUNT TITLE	DOC. NO.	POST. REF.	DEBIT	CREDIT
						1
						2
						3

3.

Cash

Prepaid Legal Fees

Legal Fees Expense

21-2 ON YOUR OWN, p. 663

Journalizing entries for deferrals

1.

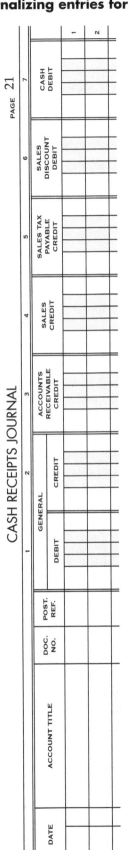

CASH RECEIPTS JOURNAL — PAGE 21

GENERAL JOURNAL — PAGE 13

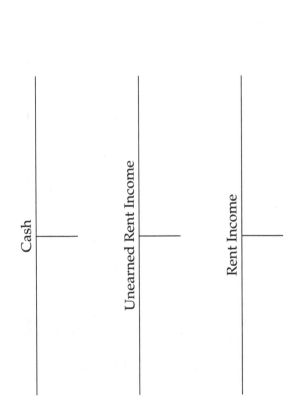

Cash

Unearned Rent Income

Rent Income

2.

CASH PAYMENTS JOURNAL

PAGE 21

					GENERAL		ACCOUNTS PAYABLE DEBIT	PURCHASES DISCOUNT CREDIT	CASH CREDIT
DATE	ACCOUNT TITLE	CK. NO.	POST. REF.	DEBIT	CREDIT				
									1

GENERAL JOURNAL

PAGE 13

DATE	ACCOUNT TITLE	DOC. NO.	POST. REF.	DEBIT	CREDIT
1					1
2					2
3					3

3.

Cash

Prepaid Rent

Rent Expense

21-1 APPLICATION PROBLEM (LO1, 2, 3, 4, 5, 6), p. 668

Journalizing entries for accruals

Spano Corporation

Unadjusted Trial Balance

December 31, 20X1

ACCOUNT TITLE	DEBIT	CREDIT
Notes Receivable	16 0 0 0 00	
Interest Receivable		
Notes Payable		18 0 0 0 00
Interest Payable		
Interest Income		2 6 1 2 00
Interest Expense	1 5 4 9 00	

1., 2.

GENERAL JOURNAL

PAGE

	DATE	ACCOUNT TITLE	DOC. NO.	POST. REF.	DEBIT	CREDIT	
1							1
2							2
3							3
4							4
5							5
6							6
7							7
8							8
9							9
10							10
11							11
12							12
13							13
14							14

3.

GENERAL JOURNAL

PAGE

	DATE	ACCOUNT TITLE	DOC. NO.	POST. REF.	DEBIT	CREDIT	
1							1
2							2
3							3
4							4
5							5
6							6
7							7
8							8
9							9
10							10
11							11
12							12

21-1 **APPLICATION PROBLEM (continued)**

4.

CASH PAYMENTS JOURNAL

PAGE 5

DATE	ACCOUNT TITLE	CK. NO.	POST. REF.	GENERAL DEBIT 1	GENERAL CREDIT 2	ACCOUNTS PAYABLE DEBIT 3	PURCHASES DISCOUNT CREDIT 4	CASH CREDIT 5
								1
								2
								3
								4
								5
								6

5.

CASH RECEIPTS JOURNAL

PAGE 7

DATE	ACCOUNT TITLE	DOC. NO.	POST. REF.	GENERAL DEBIT 1	GENERAL CREDIT 2	ACCOUNTS RECEIVABLE CREDIT 3	SALES CREDIT 4	SALES TAX PAYABLE CREDIT 5	SALES DISCOUNT DEBIT 6	CASH DEBIT 7
										1
										2
										3
										4
										5
										6

1., 2., 3., 4., 5.

Notes Receivable		
Nov. 16	16,000.00	

Notes Payable		
		Dec. 1	18,000.00

Interest Receivable		

Interest Payable		

Income Summary		

Interest Income		
		Dec. 31 Bal.	2,612.00

Interest Expense		
Dec. 31 Bal.	1,549.00	

6. Interest Income for 20X1 _____
Interest Income for 20X2 _____

7. Interest Expense for 20X1 _____
Interest Expense for 20X2 _____

21-2 APPLICATION PROBLEM (LO7, 8, 9, 10), p. 668

Journalizing entries for deferrals

1.

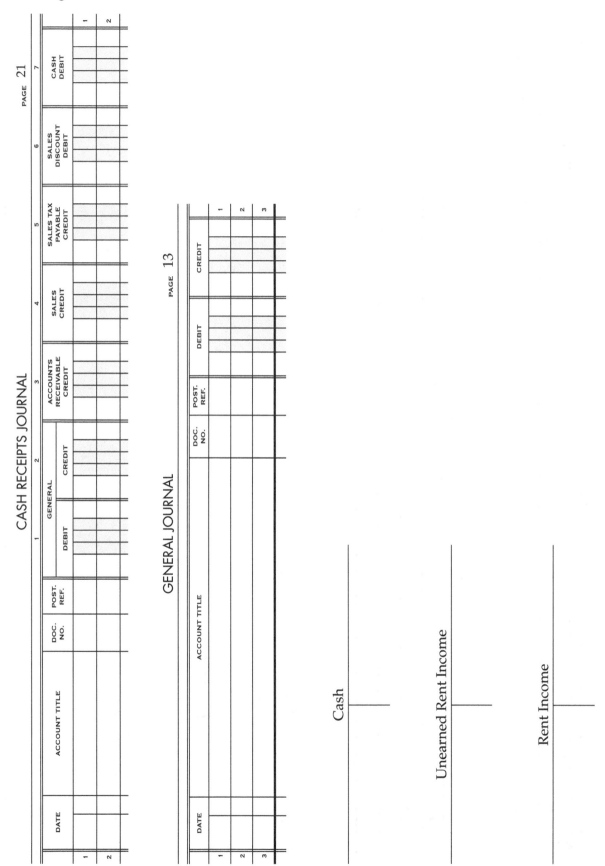

CASH RECEIPTS JOURNAL

GENERAL JOURNAL

Cash

Unearned Rent Income

Rent Income

2.

CASH PAYMENTS JOURNAL

PAGE 21

				GENERAL		ACCOUNTS PAYABLE DEBIT	PURCHASES DISCOUNT CREDIT	CASH CREDIT
DATE	ACCOUNT TITLE	CK. NO.	POST. REF.	DEBIT	CREDIT			
				1	2	3	4	5

GENERAL JOURNAL

PAGE 13

DATE	ACCOUNT TITLE	DOC. NO.	POST. REF.	DEBIT	CREDIT
1					
2					
3					

3.

Cash

Prepaid Rent

Rent Expense

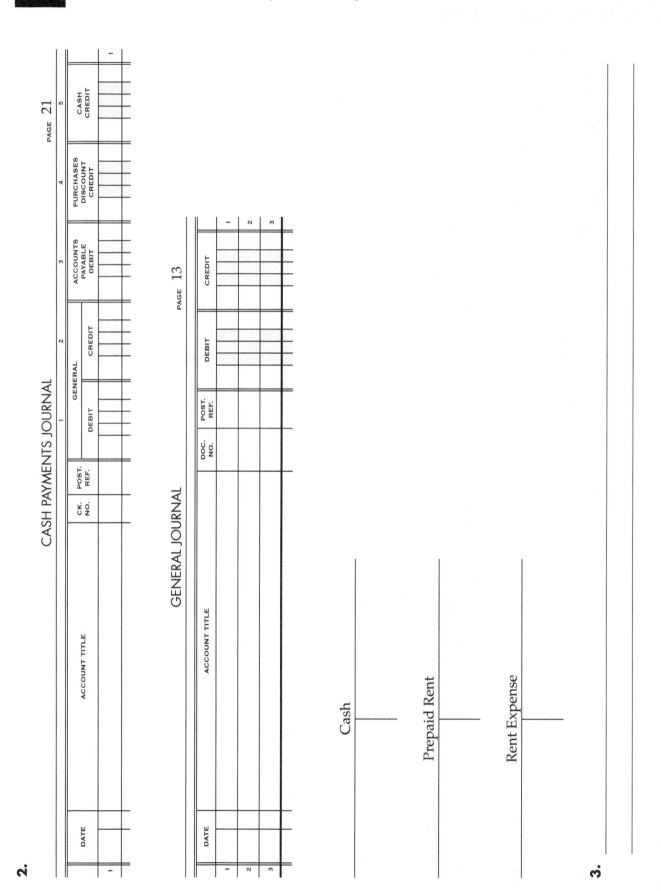

21-M MASTERY PROBLEM (LO1, 2, 3, 4, 5, 6, 7, 8), p. 669

Journalizing entries for accruals and deferrals

Figlmiller Corporation
Unadjusted Trial Balance
December 31, 20X1

ACCOUNT TITLE	DEBIT	CREDIT
Notes Receivable	13 0 0 0 00	
Interest Receivable		
Notes Payable		8 0 0 0 00
Interest Payable		
Unearned Rent Income		30 0 0 0 00
Interest Income		
Rent Income		
Interest Expense		

1., 2.

GENERAL JOURNAL

PAGE

	DATE	ACCOUNT TITLE	DOC. NO.	POST. REF.	DEBIT	CREDIT	
1							1
2							2
3							3
4							4
5							5
6							6
7							7
8							8
9							9
10							10
11							11
12							12
13							13
14							14
15							15
16							16

3.

GENERAL JOURNAL

PAGE

	DATE	ACCOUNT TITLE	DOC. NO.	POST. REF.	DEBIT	CREDIT	
1							1
2							2
3							3
4							4
5							5
6							6
7							7
8							8
9							9

21-M MASTERY PROBLEM (continued)

4.

CASH RECEIPTS JOURNAL

PAGE 7

				1 GENERAL	2 GENERAL	3 ACCOUNTS RECEIVABLE CREDIT	4 SALES CREDIT	5 SALES TAX PAYABLE CREDIT	6 SALES DISCOUNT DEBIT	7 CASH DEBIT
DATE	ACCOUNT TITLE	DOC. NO.	POST. REF.	DEBIT	CREDIT					

5.

CASH PAYMENTS JOURNAL

PAGE 5

				1 GENERAL	2 GENERAL	3 ACCOUNTS PAYABLE DEBIT	4 PURCHASES DISCOUNT CREDIT	5 CASH CREDIT
DATE	ACCOUNT TITLE	CK. NO.	POST. REF.	DEBIT	CREDIT			

1., 2., 3., 4., 5.

	Notes Receivable	
Dec. 1	13,000.00	

	Interest Receivable	

	Notes Payable	
	Nov. 16	8,000.00

	Unearned Rent Income	
	Nov. 1	30,000.00

	Interest Payable	

	Income Summary	

	Interest Income	
	Dec. 31 Bal.	0.00

	Rent Income	
	Dec. 31 Bal.	0.00

	Interest Expense	
Dec. 31 Bal.	0.00	

6. Interest Income for 20X1 _____
Interest Income for 20X2 _____

7. Interest Expense for 20X1 _____
Interest Expense for 20X2 _____

8. _____

_____

21-C   CHALLENGE PROBLEM (LO7, 8), p. 670

Journalizing entries for deferred revenue

1.

GENERAL JOURNAL   PAGE 13

	DATE		ACCOUNT TITLE	DOC. NO.	POST. REF.	DEBIT	CREDIT	
1								1
2								2
3								3
4								4
5								5

Unearned Membership Fees
_____
        Nov. 1 Bal.   300,000.00

Unearned Magazine Subscriptions
_____
        Nov. 30 Bal.   36,000.00

Membership Fees
_____

Magazine Subscriptions
_____

2. _____

_____

3. _____

_____

4. _____

_____

_____

_____

_____

_____

Name	Perfect Score	Your Score
Identifying Accounting Concepts and Practices for End-of-Fiscal-Period Work	17 Pts.	
Analyzing End-of-Fiscal-Period Entries for a Corporation	34 Pts.	
Total	51 Pts.	

Part One—Identifying Accounting Concepts and Practices for End-of-Fiscal-Period Work

Directions: Place a *T* for True or an *F* for False in the Answers column to show whether each of the following statements is true or false.

Answers

1. The unadjusted trial balance and other financial data are used to plan and record adjustments. (p. 674)   1. _____

2. Financial statements are prepared using an unadjusted trial balance. (p. 674)   2. _____

3. All accounts that need to be brought up to date are adjusted after financial statements are prepared. (p. 677)   3. _____

4. To bring the Supplies account up to date, the balance of supplies needs to be decreased by the cost of supplies used during the year. (p. 679)   4. _____

5. The tax rate for federal income tax varies depending on the amount of net income earned. (p. 680)   5. _____

6. After all adjusting entries are journalized and posted, an adjusted trial balance is prepared. (p. 682)   6. _____

7. Gains and losses from the sale of plant assets are listed before income from operations on the income statement. (p. 686)   7. _____

8. On an income statement, the difference between other revenues and other expenses is reported as a net addition or net deduction. (p. 686)   8. _____

9. If a company has issued both common and preferred stock, its statement of stockholders' equity will contain only two major sections: capital stock and retained earnings. (p. 687)   9. _____

10. Bonds Payable is an example of a long-term liability account. (p. 688)   10. _____

11. The statement of cash flows is prepared on a cash basis rather than an accrual basis. (p. 691)   11. _____

12. The purchase of office equipment for cash would be listed as a financing activity on the statement of cash flows. (p. 692)   12. _____

13. The payment of interest would be listed as a cash outflow in the operating activities section on the statement of cash flows. (p. 692)   13. _____

14. The sale of office equipment would be listed as a cash inflow in the operating activities section on the statement of cash flows. (p. 692)   14. _____

15. The payment of cash dividends would be listed as an investing activity on the statement of cash flows. (p. 692)   15. _____

16. Closing entries for a corporation are made from information in a balance sheet. (p. 700)   16. _____

17. A reversing entry is desirable if an adjusting entry creates a balance in an asset or a liability account. (p. 703)   17. _____

Part Two—Analyzing End-of-Fiscal-Period Entries for a Corporation

Directions: For each closing or reversing entry described, decide which accounts are debited and credited. Print the letter identifying your choice in the proper Answers columns. (Accounts are listed in alphabetical order.)

Account Titles	Transactions	Answers Debit	Credit
A. Cash Short and Over	1–2. Closing entry for the Sales account. (p. 700)	1. ____	2. ____
B. Depreciation Expense— Store Equipment	3–4. Closing entry for the Purchases Discount account. (p. 700)	3. ____	4. ____
C. Dividends	5–6. Closing entry for the Purchases Returns and Allowances account. (p. 700)	5. ____	6. ____
D. Dividends Payable			
E. Federal Income Tax Expense	7–8. Closing entry for the Interest Income account. (p. 700)	7. ____	8. ____
F. Federal Income Tax Payable	9–10. Closing entry for the Rent Income account. (p. 700)	9. ____	10. ____
G. Gain on Plant Assets			
H. Income Summary	11–12. Closing entry for the Gain on Plant Assets account. (p. 700)	11. ____	12. ____
I. Insurance Expense			
J. Interest Expense	13–14. Closing entry for the Sales Discount account. (p. 701)	13. ____	14. ____
K. Interest Income	15–16. Closing entry for the Purchases account. (p. 701)	15. ____	16. ____
L. Interest Payable			
M. Interest Receivable	17–18. Closing entry for the Cash Short and Over account (cash is short). (p. 701)	17. ____	18. ____
N. Loss on Plant Assets			
O. Purchases	19–20. Closing entry for the Depreciation Expense— Store Equipment account. (p. 701)	19. ____	20. ____
P. Purchases Discount	21–22. Closing entry for the Federal Income Tax Expense account. (p. 701)	21. ____	22. ____
Q. Purchases Returns and Allowances			
	23–24. Closing entry for the Income Summary account (net income). (p. 702)	23. ____	24. ____
R. Rent Income	25–26. Closing entry for the Income Summary account (net loss). (p. 702)	25. ____	26. ____
S. Retained Earnings			
T. Sales	27–28. Closing entry for the Dividends account. (p. 702)	27. ____	28. ____
U. Sales Discount			
	29–30. Reversing entry for accrued interest income. (p. 703)	29. ____	30. ____
	31–32. Reversing entry for accrued interest expense. (p. 703)	31. ____	32. ____
	33–34. Reversing entry for the Federal Income Tax Payable account. (p. 703)	33. ____	34. ____

22-1 WORK TOGETHER, p. 684

Recording adjusting entries and preparing an adjusted trial balance

Travel Lite Corporation

Unadjusted Trial Balance

December 31, 20--

ACCOUNT TITLE	DEBIT	CREDIT
Cash	45 0 2 6 12	
Petty Cash	1 5 0 00	
Accounts Receivable	35 0 4 7 05	
Allowance for Uncollectible Accounts		2 2 32
Notes Receivable	5 4 7 6 00	
Interest Receivable	—	
Merchandise Inventory	32 1 5 8 15	
Supplies	1 2 7 6 04	
Prepaid Insurance	4 5 3 5 80	
Equipment	25 0 6 9 60	
Accumulated Depreciation—Equipment		6 5 4 6 20
Accounts Payable		16 0 5 8 09
Sales Tax Payable		3 3 2 6 30
Notes Payable		7 2 0 0 00
Interest Payable		—
Unearned Rent Income		4 0 0 0 00
Employee Income Tax Payable		8 2 6 20
Social Security Tax Payable		7 7 4 60
Medicare Tax Payable		1 7 8 76
Medical Insurance Payable		3 5 1 30
Unemployment Tax Payable—State		1 1 2 86
Unemployment Tax Payable—Federal		1 6 72
Federal Income Tax Payable		—
Dividends Payable		5 4 0 0 00
Bonds Payable		10 0 0 0 00
Capital Stock—Common		5 0 0 0 00
Paid-in Capital in Excess of Par—Common		20 0 0 0 00
Capital Stock—Preferred		5 0 0 0 00

(Note: Unadjusted trial balance is continued on next page.)

Travel Lite Corporation

Unadjusted Trial Balance (Concluded)

December 31, 20--

ACCOUNT TITLE	DEBIT	CREDIT
Paid-in Capital in Excess of Par—Preferred		
Retained Earnings		19 6 2 0 77
Dividends	21 6 0 0 00	
Income Summary		
Sales		587 9 3 4 15
Sales Discount	1 0 1 0 40	
Sales Returns and Allowances	4 1 7 3 60	
Purchases	388 7 3 2 40	
Purchases Discount		2 7 4 1 80
Purchases Returns and Allowances		1 3 5 8 07
Advertising Expense	7 9 7 3 50	
Cash Short and Over	4 58	
Credit Card Fee Expense	5 0 3 3 47	
Depreciation Expense—Equipment		
Insurance Expense		
Miscellaneous Expense	4 3 4 1 10	
Payroll Taxes Expense	7 4 8 3 00	
Rent Expense	14 4 5 7 50	
Repairs Expense	1 7 4 2 50	
Salary Expense	79 4 8 2 00	
Supplies Expense		
Uncollectible Accounts Expense		
Utilities Expense	4 3 3 0 50	
Federal Income Tax Expense	6 6 5 0 00	
Interest Income		4 4 7 24
Rent Income		
Gain on Plant Assets		5 5 00
Interest Expense	1 0 9 3 07	
Loss on Plant Assets	1 2 4 00	
Totals	696 9 7 0 38	696 9 7 0 38

22-1 WORK TOGETHER (continued)

1., 4., 5.

GENERAL JOURNAL   PAGE 12

	DATE		ACCOUNT TITLE	DOC. NO.	POST. REF.	DEBIT	CREDIT	
1								1
2								2
3								3
4								4
5								5
6								6
7								7
8								8
9								9
10								10
11								11
12								12
13								13
14								14
15								15
16								16
17								17
18								18
19								19
20								20

2., 5.

Allowance for Uncollectible Accounts		
	Balance	22.32
	Balance	3,697.32

Income Summary

Interest Receivable

Depreciation Expense—Equipment

Merchandise Inventory		
Balance	32,158.15	
Balance	45,058.15	

Insurance Expense

Supplies		
Balance	1,276.04	
Balance	126.00	

Supplies Expense

22-1 WORK TOGETHER (continued)

Prepaid Insurance

Balance	4,535.80	
Balance	1,535.80	

Uncollectible Accounts Expense

Accumulated Depreciation—Equipment

		Balance	6,546.20
		Balance	8,796.20

Federal Income Tax Expense

Balance	6,650.00	
Balance	14,171.44	

Interest Payable

Interest Income

		Balance	447.24
		Balance	584.74

Unearned Rent Income

		Balance	4,000.00
		Balance	3,000.00

Rent Income

Federal Income Tax Payable

Interest Expense

Balance	1,093.07	
Balance	1,370.65	

3., 6.

Adjusted Trial Balance

ACCOUNT TITLE	DEBIT	CREDIT
Cash	45 0 2 6 12	
Petty Cash	1 5 0 00	
Accounts Receivable	35 0 4 7 05	
Allowance for Uncollectible Accounts		
Notes Receivable	5 4 7 6 00	
Interest Receivable		
Merchandise Inventory		
Supplies		
Prepaid Insurance		
Equipment	25 0 6 9 60	
Accumulated Depreciation—Equipment		
Accounts Payable		16 0 5 8 09
Sales Tax Payable		3 3 2 6 30
Notes Payable		7 2 0 0 00
Interest Payable		
Unearned Rent Income		
Employee Income Tax Payable		8 2 6 20
Social Security Tax Payable		7 7 4 60
Medicare Tax Payable		1 7 8 76
Medical Insurance Payable		3 5 1 30
Unemployment Tax Payable—State		1 1 2 86
Unemployment Tax Payable—Federal		1 6 72
Federal Income Tax Payable		
Dividends Payable		5 4 0 0 00
Bonds Payable		10 0 0 0 00
Capital Stock—Common		5 0 0 0 00
Paid-in Capital in Excess of Par—Common		20 0 0 0 00
Capital Stock—Preferred		5 0 0 0 00

(Note: Adjusted trial balance is continued on next page.)

22-1 WORK TOGETHER (concluded)

Adjusted Trial Balance (Concluded)

ACCOUNT TITLE	DEBIT	CREDIT
Paid-in Capital in Excess of Par—Preferred		
Retained Earnings		19 6 2 0 77
Dividends	21 6 0 0 00	
Income Summary		
Sales		587 9 3 4 15
Sales Discount	1 0 1 0 40	
Sales Returns and Allowances	4 1 7 3 60	
Purchases	388 7 3 2 40	
Purchases Discount		2 7 4 1 80
Purchases Returns and Allowances		1 3 5 8 07
Advertising Expense	7 9 7 3 50	
Cash Short and Over	4 58	
Credit Card Fee Expense	5 0 3 3 47	
Depreciation Expense—Equipment		
Insurance Expense		
Miscellaneous Expense	4 3 4 1 10	
Payroll Taxes Expense	7 4 8 3 00	
Rent Expense	14 4 5 7 50	
Repairs Expense	1 7 4 2 50	
Salary Expense	79 4 8 2 00	
Supplies Expense		
Uncollectible Accounts Expense		
Utilities Expense	4 3 3 0 50	
Federal Income Tax Expense		
Interest Income		
Rent Income		
Gain on Plant Assets		5 5 00
Interest Expense		
Loss on Plant Assets	1 2 4 00	

ON YOUR OWN, p. 684

Recording adjusting entries and preparing an adjusted trial balance

Williams Corporation

Unadjusted Trial Balance

December 31, 20--

ACCOUNT TITLE	DEBIT	CREDIT
Cash	8 4 2 7 05	
Petty Cash	1 5 0 00	
Accounts Receivable	41 2 4 1 61	
Allowance for Uncollectible Accounts		1 4 0 00
Notes Receivable	4 0 0 0 00	
Interest Receivable		
Merchandise Inventory	97 9 4 2 13	
Supplies	4 6 0 9 12	
Prepaid Insurance	7 9 0 0 00	
Equipment	49 5 3 6 38	
Accumulated Depreciation—Equipment		19 1 8 3 25
Accounts Payable		9 2 4 4 65
Sales Tax Payable		2 9 8 8 00
Notes Payable		4 5 0 0 00
Interest Payable		
Unearned Rent Income		8 0 0 0 00
Employee Income Tax Payable		1 1 2 8 00
Social Security Tax Payable		1 0 6 0 67
Medicare Tax Payable		2 5 6 33
Medical Insurance Payable		3 3 6 00
Unemployment Tax Payable—State		1 4 6 40
Unemployment Tax Payable—Federal		2 2 80
Federal Income Tax Payable		
Dividends Payable		2 5 0 0 00
Bonds Payable		15 0 0 0 00
Capital Stock—Common		15 0 0 0 00
Paid-in Capital in Excess of Par—Common		5 0 0 0 00
Capital Stock—Preferred		10 0 0 0 00

(Note: Unadjusted trial balance is continued on next page.)

22-1 **ON YOUR OWN (continued)**

Williams Corporation

Unadjusted Trial Balance (Concluded)

December 31, 20--

ACCOUNT TITLE	DEBIT	CREDIT
Paid-in Capital in Excess of Par—Preferred		
Retained Earnings		20 0 7 1 08
Dividends	10 0 0 0 00	
Income Summary		
Sales		1282 2 4 1 65
Sales Discount	6 2 4 2 64	
Sales Returns and Allowances	11 4 4 7 05	
Purchases	819 4 0 8 57	
Purchases Discount		3 9 4 5 59
Purchases Returns and Allowances		3 0 7 4 10
Advertising Expense	19 0 5 7 10	
Cash Short and Over	7 66	
Credit Card Fee Expense	9 0 6 1 05	
Depreciation Expense—Equipment		
Insurance Expense		
Miscellaneous Expense	14 7 4 2 63	
Payroll Taxes Expense	16 0 7 4 12	
Rent Expense	27 0 0 0 00	
Repairs Expense	6 2 4 3 96	
Salary Expense	210 7 9 2 50	
Supplies Expense		
Uncollectible Accounts Expense		
Utilities Expense	11 5 9 9 95	
Federal Income Tax Expense	28 0 0 0 00	
Interest Income		3 1 5 50
Rent Income		
Gain on Plant Assets		1 2 2 9 00
Interest Expense	8 9 0 00	
Loss on Plant Assets	1 0 0 9 50	
Totals	1405 3 8 3 02	1405 3 8 3 02

1., 4., 5.

GENERAL JOURNAL

	DATE		ACCOUNT TITLE	DOC. NO.	POST. REF.	DEBIT	CREDIT	
1								1
2								2
3								3
4								4
5								5
6								6
7								7
8								8
9								9
10								10
11								11
12								12
13								13
14								14
15								15
16								16
17								17
18								18
19								19
20								20

22-1 **ON YOUR OWN (continued)**

2., 5.

Allowance for Uncollectible Accounts	
	Balance 140.00
	Balance 3,796.00

Income Summary

Interest Receivable

Depreciation Expense—Equipment

Merchandise Inventory	
Balance 97,942.13	
Balance 98,996.13	

Insurance Expense

Supplies	
Balance 4,609.12	
Balance 401.25	

Supplies Expense

Prepaid Insurance

Balance	7,900.00		
Balance	600.00		

Uncollectible Accounts Expense

Accumulated Depreciation—Equipment

		Balance	19,183.25
		Balance	26,528.25

Federal Income Tax Expense

Balance	28,000.00		
Balance	29,154.65		

Interest Payable

Interest Income

		Balance	315.50
		Balance	395.50

Unearned Rent Income

		Balance	8,000.00
		Balance	6,000.00

Rent Income

Federal Income Tax Payable

Interest Expense

Balance	890.00		
Balance	1,040.00		

22-1 ON YOUR OWN (continued)

3., 6.

Adjusted Trial Balance

ACCOUNT TITLE	DEBIT	CREDIT
Cash	8 4 2 7 05	
Petty Cash	1 5 0 00	
Accounts Receivable	41 2 4 1 61	
Allowance for Uncollectible Accounts		
Notes Receivable	4 0 0 0 00	
Interest Receivable		
Merchandise Inventory		
Supplies		
Prepaid Insurance		
Equipment	49 5 3 6 38	
Accumulated Depreciation—Equipment		
Accounts Payable		9 2 4 4 65
Sales Tax Payable		2 9 8 8 00
Notes Payable		4 5 0 0 00
Interest Payable		
Unearned Rent Income		
Employee Income Tax Payable		1 1 2 8 00
Social Security Tax Payable		1 0 6 0 67
Medicare Tax Payable		2 5 6 33
Medical Insurance Payable		3 3 6 00
Unemployment Tax Payable—State		1 4 6 40
Unemployment Tax Payable—Federal		2 2 80
Federal Income Tax Payable		
Dividends Payable		2 5 0 0 00
Bonds Payable		15 0 0 0 00
Capital Stock—Common		15 0 0 0 00
Paid-in Capital in Excess of Par—Common		5 0 0 0 00
Capital Stock—Preferred		10 0 0 0 00

(Note: Adjusted trial balance is continued on next page.)

Adjusted Trial Balance (Concluded)

ACCOUNT TITLE	DEBIT	CREDIT
Paid-in Capital in Excess of Par—Preferred		
Retained Earnings		20 0 7 1 08
Dividends	10 0 0 0 00	
Income Summary		
Sales		1282 2 4 1 65
Sales Discount	6 2 4 2 64	
Sales Returns and Allowances	11 4 4 7 05	
Purchases	819 4 0 8 57	
Purchases Discount		3 9 4 5 59
Purchases Returns and Allowances		3 0 7 4 10
Advertising Expense	19 0 5 7 10	
Cash Short and Over	7 66	
Credit Card Fee Expense	9 0 6 1 05	
Depreciation Expense—Equipment		
Insurance Expense		
Miscellaneous Expense	14 7 4 2 63	
Payroll Taxes Expense	16 0 7 4 12	
Rent Expense	27 0 0 0 00	
Repairs Expense	6 2 4 3 96	
Salary Expense	210 7 9 2 50	
Supplies Expense		
Uncollectible Accounts Expense		
Utilities Expense	11 5 9 9 95	
Federal Income Tax Expense		
Interest Income		
Rent Income		
Gain on Plant Assets		1 2 2 9 00
Interest Expense		
Loss on Plant Assets	1 0 0 9 50	

22-2 WORK TOGETHER, p. 690

Preparing an income statement, statement of stockholders' equity, and balance sheet for a corporation

1.

Income Statement

		% OF SALES
Operating Revenue:		
Sales		
Less: Sales Discount		
Sales Returns and Allowances		
Net Sales		
Cost of Merchandise Sold:		
Merchandise Inventory, January 1, 20--		
Purchases		
Less: Purchases Discount		
Purchases Returns and Allowances		
Net Purchases		
Total Cost of Merchandise Available for Sale		
Less Merchandise Inventory, December 31, 20--		
Cost of Merchandise Sold		
Gross Profit		
Operating Expenses:		
Advertising Expense		
Cash Short and Over		
Credit Card Fee Expense		
Depreciation Expense—Equipment		
Insurance Expense		
Miscellaneous Expense		
Payroll Taxes Expense		
Rent Expense		
Repairs Expense		
Salary Expense		
Supplies Expense		
Uncollectible Accounts Expense		
Utilities Expense		
Total Operating Expenses		
Income from Operations		
Other Revenue:		
Interest Income		
Rent Income		
Gain on Plant Assets		
Total Other Income		
Other Expenses:		
Interest Expense		
Loss on Plant Assets		
Total Other Expenses		
Net Addition		
Net Income before Federal Income Tax		
Less Federal Income Tax Expense		
Net Income after Federal Income Tax		

2.

Statement of Stockholders' Equity

Capital Stock—Common:					
$1.00 Par Value					
January 1, 20--, 4,500 Shares Issued					
Issued during Current Year, 500 Shares					
Balance, December 31, 20--, 5,000 Shares Issued					
Paid-in Capital in Excess of Par—Common:					
Balance, January 1, 20--					
Issued during Current Year					
Balance, December 31, 20--					
Capital Stock—Preferred:					
$10.00 Par Value, 5%					
January 1, 20--, 0 Shares Issued					
Issued during Current Year, 500 Shares					
Balance, December 31, 20--, 500 Shares Issued					
Retained Earnings:					
Balance, January 1, 20--					
Net Income after Federal Income Tax for 20--					
Less Dividends Declared during 20--					
Net Increase during 20--					
Balance, December 31, 20--					
Total Stockholders' Equity, December 31, 20--					

22-2 WORK TOGETHER (concluded)

3.

Balance Sheet

Assets													
Current Assets:													
Cash													
Petty Cash													
Accounts Receivable													
Less Allowance for Uncollectible Accounts													
Notes Receivable													
Interest Receivable													
Merchandise Inventory													
Supplies													
Prepaid Insurance													
Total Current Assets													
Plant Assets:													
Equipment													
Less Accumulated Depreciation—Equipment													
Total Plant Assets													
Total Assets													
Liabilities													
Current Liabilities:													
Accounts Payable													
Sales Tax Payable													
Notes Payable													
Interest Payable													
Unearned Rent Income													
Employee Income Tax Payable													
Social Security Tax Payable													
Medicare Tax Payable													
Medical Insurance Payable													
Unemployment Tax Payable—State													
Unemployment Tax Payable—Federal													
Federal Income Tax Payable													
Dividends Payable													
Total Current Liabilities													
Long-term Liabilities:													
Bonds Payable													
Total Long-term Liabilities													
Total Liabilities													
Stockholders' Equity													
Capital Stock—Common													
Paid-in Capital in Excess of Par—Common													
Capital Stock—Preferred													
Retained Earnings													
Total Stockholders' Equity													
Total Liabilities and Stockholders' Equity													

Preparing an income statement, statement of stockholders' equity, and balance sheet for a corporation

1.

Income Statement

		% OF SALES
Operating Revenue:		
Sales		
Less: Sales Discount		
Sales Returns and Allowances		
Net Sales		
Cost of Merchandise Sold:		
Merchandise Inventory, January 1, 20--		
Purchases		
Less: Purchases Discount		
Purchases Returns and Allowances		
Net Purchases		
Total Cost of Merchandise Available for Sale		
Less Merchandise Inventory, December 31, 20--		
Cost of Merchandise Sold		
Gross Profit		
Operating Expenses:		
Advertising Expense		
Cash Short and Over		
Credit Card Fee Expense		
Depreciation Expense—Equipment		
Insurance Expense		
Miscellaneous Expense		
Payroll Taxes Expense		
Rent Expense		
Repairs Expense		
Salary Expense		
Supplies Expense		
Uncollectible Accounts Expense		
Utilities Expense		
Total Operating Expenses		
Income from Operations		
Other Revenue:		
Interest Income		
Rent Income		
Gain on Plant Assets		
Total Other Income		
Other Expenses:		
Interest Expense		
Loss on Plant Assets		
Total Other Expenses		
Net Addition		
Net Income before Federal Income Tax		
Less Federal Income Tax Expense		
Net Income after Federal Income Tax		

22-2 **ON YOUR OWN (continued)**

2.

Statement of Stockholders' Equity

Capital Stock—Common:					
$5.00 Par Value					
January 1, 20--, 2,000 Shares Issued					
Issued during Current Year, 1,000 Shares					
Balance, December 31, 20--, 3,000 Shares Issued					
Paid-in Capital in Excess of Par—Common:					
Balance, January 1, 20--					
Issued during Current Year					
Balance, December 31, 20--					
Capital Stock—Preferred:					
$10.00 Par Value, 5%					
January 1, 20--, 0 Shares Issued					
Issued during Current Year, 1,000 Shares					
Balance, December 31, 20--, 1,000 Shares Issued					
Retained Earnings:					
Balance, January 1, 20--					
Net Income after Federal Income Tax for 20--					
Less Dividends Declared during 20--					
Net Increase during 20--					
Balance, December 31, 20--					
Total Stockholders' Equity, December 31, 20--					

3.

Balance Sheet						

Assets				
Current Assets:				
Cash				
Petty Cash				
Accounts Receivable				
Less Allowance for Uncollectible Accounts				
Notes Receivable				
Interest Receivable				
Merchandise Inventory				
Supplies				
Prepaid Insurance				
Total Current Assets				
Plant Assets:				
Equipment				
Less Accumulated Depreciation—Equipment				
Total Plant Assets				
Total Assets				
Liabilities				
Current Liabilities:				
Accounts Payable				
Sales Tax Payable				
Notes Payable				
Interest Payable				
Unearned Rent Income				
Employee Income Tax Payable				
Social Security Tax Payable				
Medicare Tax Payable				
Medical Insurance Payable				
Unemployment Tax Payable—State				
Unemployment Tax Payable—Federal				
Federal Income Tax Payable				
Dividends Payable				
Total Current Liabilities				
Long-term Liabilities:				
Bonds Payable				
Total Long-term Liabilities				
Total Liabilities				
Stockholders' Equity				
Capital Stock—Common				
Paid-in Capital in Excess of Par—Common				
Capital Stock—Preferred				
Retained Earnings				
Total Stockholders' Equity				
Total Liabilities and Stockholders' Equity				

Name _____ Date _____ Class _____

Preparing a statement of cash flows for a corporation

Statement of Cash Flows

Preparing a statement of cash flows for a corporation

Statement of Cash Flows

22-4 **WORK TOGETHER, p. 706**

Journalizing closing and reversing entries for a corporation

1.

GENERAL JOURNAL   PAGE 13

	DATE	ACCOUNT TITLE	DOC. NO.	POST. REF.	DEBIT	CREDIT	
1							1
2							2
3							3
4							4
5							5
6							6
7							7
8							8
9							9
10							10
11							11
12							12
13							13
14							14
15							15
16							16
17							17
18							18
19							19
20							20
21							21
22							22
23							23
24							24
25							25
26							26
27							27
28							28
29							29
30							30
31							31
32							32

2.

GENERAL JOURNAL

PAGE 14

	DATE		ACCOUNT TITLE	DOC. NO.	POST. REF.	DEBIT	CREDIT	
1								1
2								2
3								3
4								4
5								5
6								6
7								7
8								8
9								9
10								10
11								11
12								12
13								13
14								14
15								15
16								16
17								17
18								18
19								19
20								20
21								21
22								22
23								23
24								24
25								25
26								26
27								27
28								28
29								29
30								30
31								31
32								32

22-4 **ON YOUR OWN, p. 706**

Journalizing closing and reversing entries for a corporation

1.

GENERAL JOURNAL

PAGE

	DATE	ACCOUNT TITLE	DOC. NO.	POST. REF.	DEBIT	CREDIT	
1							1
2							2
3							3
4							4
5							5
6							6
7							7
8							8
9							9
10							10
11							11
12							12
13							13
14							14
15							15
16							16
17							17
18							18
19							19
20							20
21							21
22							22
23							23
24							24
25							25
26							26
27							27
28							28
29							29
30							30
31							31
32							32

2.

GENERAL JOURNAL

PAGE

	DATE		ACCOUNT TITLE	DOC. NO.	POST. REF.	DEBIT	CREDIT	
1								1
2								2
3								3
4								4
5								5
6								6
7								7
8								8
9								9
10								10
11								11
12								12
13								13
14								14
15								15
16								16
17								17
18								18
19								19
20								20
21								21
22								22
23								23
24								24
25								25
26								26
27								27
28								28
29								29
30								30
31								31
32								32

22-1 APPLICATION PROBLEM (LO1), p. 709

Recording adjusting entries and preparing an adjusted trial balance

Handy Hardware Corporation

Unadjusted Trial Balance

December 31, 20--

ACCOUNT TITLE	DEBIT	CREDIT
Cash	37 6 9 7 16	
Petty Cash	2 0 0 00	
Accounts Receivable	114 3 7 5 60	
Allowance for Uncollectible Accounts		1 3 2 96
Notes Receivable	11 6 9 7 60	
Interest Receivable		
Merchandise Inventory	157 7 1 6 00	
Supplies	9 9 7 5 40	
Prepaid Insurance	17 8 9 6 00	
Equipment	88 3 7 1 20	
Accumulated Depreciation—Equipment		26 7 1 8 00
Accounts Payable		16 7 4 5 60
Sales Tax Payable		5 6 9 4 00
Notes Payable		60 0 0 0 00
Interest Payable		
Unearned Rent Income		12 0 0 0 00
Employee Income Tax Payable		2 9 7 2 60
Social Security Tax Payable		2 4 1 9 62
Medicare Tax Payable		5 5 8 38
Medical Insurance Payable		6 9 7 60
Unemployment Tax Payable—State		3 9 0 00
Unemployment Tax Payable—Federal		5 8 50
Federal Income Tax Payable		
Dividends Payable		10 0 0 0 00
Bonds Payable		18 0 0 0 00
Capital Stock—Common		20 0 0 0 00
Paid-in Capital in Excess of Par—Common		50 0 0 0 00
Capital Stock—Preferred		30 0 0 0 00

(Note: Unadjusted trial balance is continued on next page.)

Handy Hardware Corporation

Unadjusted Trial Balance (Concluded)

December 31, 20--

ACCOUNT TITLE	DEBIT	CREDIT
Paid-in Capital in Excess of Par—Preferred		
Retained Earnings		61 6 4 6 36
Dividends	40 0 0 0 00	
Income Summary		
Sales		1967 6 7 4 40
Sales Discount	3 7 8 9 00	
Sales Returns and Allowances	9 1 6 7 00	
Purchases	1394 6 3 7 00	
Purchases Discount		8 4 3 1 00
Purchases Returns and Allowances		3 6 9 6 94
Advertising Expense	18 9 6 7 60	
Cash Short and Over	2 0 40	
Credit Card Fee Expense	16 9 6 5 80	
Depreciation Expense—Equipment		
Insurance Expense		
Miscellaneous Expense	18 3 6 9 60	
Payroll Taxes Expense	25 6 9 6 00	
Rent Expense	30 0 0 0 00	
Repairs Expense	8 2 0 9 60	
Salary Expense	250 9 6 6 40	
Supplies Expense		
Uncollectible Accounts Expense		
Utilities Expense	14 3 1 7 80	
Federal Income Tax Expense	24 0 0 0 00	
Interest Income		4 5 4 00
Rent Income		
Gain on Plant Assets		1 4 3 0 00
Interest Expense	6 3 1 6 80	
Loss on Plant Assets	3 6 8 00	
Totals	2299 7 1 9 96	2299 7 1 9 96

22-1 **APPLICATION PROBLEM (continued)**

1., 4., 5.

GENERAL JOURNAL PAGE 12

	DATE	ACCOUNT TITLE	DOC. NO.	POST. REF.	DEBIT	CREDIT	
1							1
2							2
3							3
4							4
5							5
6							6
7							7
8							8
9							9
10							10
11							11
12							12
13							13
14							14
15							15
16							16
17							17
18							18
19							19
20							20

2., 5.

Allowance for Uncollectible Accounts

		Balance	132.96
		Balance	13,832.96

Income Summary

Interest Receivable

Depreciation Expense—Equipment

Merchandise Inventory

Balance	157,716.00		
Balance	162,569.00		

Insurance Expense

Supplies

Balance	9,975.40		
Balance	3,695.00		

Supplies Expense

22-1 **APPLICATION PROBLEM (continued)**

Prepaid Insurance	
Balance	17,896.00
Balance	8,360.00

Uncollectible Accounts Expense	

Accumulated Depreciation—Equipment	
Balance	26,718.00
Balance	39,752.00

Federal Income Tax Expense	
Balance	24,000.00
Balance	41,838.90

Interest Payable	

Interest Income	
Balance	454.00
Balance	1,084.00

Unearned Rent Income	
Balance	12,000.00
Balance	8,000.00

Rent Income	

Federal Income Tax Payable	

Interest Expense	
Balance	6,316.80
Balance	6,916.80

3., 6.

Adjusted Trial Balance

ACCOUNT TITLE	DEBIT	CREDIT
Cash	37 6 9 7 16	
Petty Cash	2 0 0 00	
Accounts Receivable	114 3 7 5 60	
Allowance for Uncollectible Accounts		
Notes Receivable	11 6 9 7 60	
Interest Receivable		
Merchandise Inventory		
Supplies		
Prepaid Insurance		
Equipment	88 3 7 1 20	
Accumulated Depreciation—Equipment		
Accounts Payable		16 7 4 5 60
Sales Tax Payable		5 6 9 4 00
Notes Payable		60 0 0 0 00
Interest Payable		
Unearned Rent Income		
Employee Income Tax Payable		2 9 7 2 60
Social Security Tax Payable		2 4 1 9 62
Medicare Tax Payable		5 5 8 38
Medical Insurance Payable		6 9 7 60
Unemployment Tax Payable—State		3 9 0 00
Unemployment Tax Payable—Federal		5 8 50
Federal Income Tax Payable		
Dividends Payable		10 0 0 0 00
Bonds Payable		18 0 0 0 00
Capital Stock—Common		20 0 0 0 00
Paid-in Capital in Excess of Par—Common		50 0 0 0 00
Capital Stock—Preferred		30 0 0 0 00

(Note: Adjusted trial balance is continued on next page.)

22-1 APPLICATION PROBLEM (concluded)

Adjusted Trial Balance (Concluded)

ACCOUNT TITLE	DEBIT	CREDIT
Paid-in Capital in Excess of Par—Preferred		
Retained Earnings		61 6 4 6 36
Dividends	40 0 0 0 00	
Income Summary		
Sales		1967 6 7 4 40
Sales Discount	3 7 8 9 00	
Sales Returns and Allowances	9 1 6 7 00	
Purchases	1394 6 3 7 00	
Purchases Discount		8 4 3 1 00
Purchases Returns and Allowances		3 6 9 6 94
Advertising Expense	18 9 6 7 60	
Cash Short and Over	2 0 40	
Credit Card Fee Expense	16 9 6 5 80	
Depreciation Expense—Equipment		
Insurance Expense		
Miscellaneous Expense	18 3 6 9 60	
Payroll Taxes Expense	25 6 9 6 00	
Rent Expense	30 0 0 0 00	
Repairs Expense	8 2 0 9 60	
Salary Expense	250 9 6 6 40	
Supplies Expense		
Uncollectible Accounts Expense		
Utilities Expense	14 3 1 7 80	
Federal Income Tax Expense		
Interest Income		
Rent Income		
Gain on Plant Assets		1 4 3 0 00
Interest Expense		
Loss on Plant Assets	3 6 8 00	

APPLICATION PROBLEM (LO2, 3, 4), p. 709

Preparing an income statement, statement of stockholders' equity, and balance sheet for a corporation

1.

Income Statement

		% OF SALES
Operating Revenue:		
Sales		
Less: Sales Discount		
Sales Returns and Allowances		
Net Sales		
Cost of Merchandise Sold:		
Merchandise Inventory, January 1, 20--		
Purchases		
Less: Purchases Discount		
Purchases Returns and Allowances		
Net Purchases		
Total Cost of Merchandise Available for Sale		
Less Merchandise Inventory, December 31, 20--		
Cost of Merchandise Sold		
Gross Profit		
Operating Expenses:		
Advertising Expense		
Cash Short and Over		
Credit Card Fee Expense		
Depreciation Expense—Equipment		
Insurance Expense		
Miscellaneous Expense		
Payroll Taxes Expense		
Rent Expense		
Repairs Expense		
Salary Expense		
Supplies Expense		
Uncollectible Accounts Expense		
Utilities Expense		
Total Operating Expenses		
Income from Operations		
Other Revenue:		
Interest Income		
Rent Income		
Gain on Plant Assets		
Total Other Income		
Other Expenses:		
Interest Expense		
Loss on Plant Assets		
Total Other Expenses		
Net Deduction		
Net Income before Federal Income Tax		
Less Federal Income Tax Expense		
Net Income after Federal Income Tax		

22-2 APPLICATION PROBLEM (continued)

2.

Statement of Stockholders' Equity

Capital Stock—Common:					
$1.00 Par Value					
January 1, 20--, 15,000 Shares Issued					
Issued during Current Year, 5,000 Shares					
Balance, December 31, 20--, 20,000 Shares Issued					
Paid-in Capital in Excess of Par—Common:					
Balance, January 1, 20--					
Issued during Current Year					
Balance, December 31, 20--					
Capital Stock—Preferred:					
$30.00 Par Value, 5%					
January 1, 20--, 0 Shares Issued					
Issued during Current Year, 1,000 Shares					
Balance, December 31, 20--, 1,000 Shares Issued					
Retained Earnings:					
Balance, January 1, 20--					
Net Income after Federal Income Tax for 20--					
Less Dividends Declared during 20--					
Net Increase during 20--					
Balance, December 31, 20--					
Total Stockholders' Equity, December 31, 20--					

3.

Balance Sheet														
Assets														
Current Assets:														
Cash														
Petty Cash														
Accounts Receivable														
Less Allowance for Uncollectible Accounts														
Notes Receivable														
Interest Receivable														
Merchandise Inventory														
Supplies														
Prepaid Insurance														
Total Current Assets														
Plant Assets:														
Equipment														
Less Accumulated Depreciation—Equipment														
Total Plant Assets														
Total Assets														
Liabilities														
Current Liabilities:														
Accounts Payable														
Sales Tax Payable														
Notes Payable														
Interest Payable														
Unearned Rent Income														
Employee Income Tax Payable														
Social Security Tax Payable														
Medicare Tax Payable														
Medical Insurance Payable														
Unemployment Tax Payable—State														
Unemployment Tax Payable—Federal														
Federal Income Tax Payable														
Dividends Payable														
Total Current Liabilities														
Long-term Liabilities:														
Bonds Payable														
Total Long-term Liabilities														
Total Liabilities														
Stockholders' Equity														
Capital Stock—Common														
Paid-in Capital in Excess of Par—Common														
Capital Stock—Preferred														
Retained Earnings														
Total Stockholders' Equity														
Total Liabilities and Stockholders' Equity														

22-3 **APPLICATION PROBLEM (LO5), p. 709**

Preparing a statement of cash flows for a corporation

Statement of Cash Flows

Journalizing closing and reversing entries for a corporation

1.

GENERAL JOURNAL

PAGE

	DATE		ACCOUNT TITLE	DOC. NO.	POST. REF.	DEBIT	CREDIT	
1								1
2								2
3								3
4								4
5								5
6								6
7								7
8								8
9								9
10								10
11								11
12								12
13								13
14								14
15								15
16								16
17								17
18								18
19								19
20								20
21								21
22								22
23								23
24								24
25								25
26								26
27								27
28								28
29								29
30								30
31								31
32								32

22-4 APPLICATION PROBLEM (concluded)

2.

GENERAL JOURNAL

PAGE ____

	DATE		ACCOUNT TITLE	DOC. NO.	POST. REF.	DEBIT	CREDIT	
1								1
2								2
3								3
4								4
5								5
6								6
7								7
8								8
9								9
10								10
11								11
12								12
13								13
14								14
15								15
16								16
17								17
18								18
19								19
20								20
21								21
22								22
23								23
24								24
25								25
26								26
27								27
28								28
29								29
30								30
31								31
32								32

Journalizing adjustments, preparing financial statements, and journalizing end-of-fiscal-period entries for a corporation

Ramel Corporation

Unadjusted Trial Balance

December 31, 20--

ACCOUNT TITLE	DEBIT	CREDIT
Cash	55 0 3 6 50	
Petty Cash	2 5 0 00	
Accounts Receivable	251 6 9 6 50	
Allowance for Uncollectible Accounts		3 2 0 00
Notes Receivable	8 0 0 0 00	
Interest Receivable	——	
Merchandise Inventory	576 6 3 6 16	
Supplies	12 9 6 2 56	
Prepaid Insurance	28 0 0 0 00	
Office Equipment	58 2 9 6 44	
Accumulated Depreciation—Office Equipment		17 4 2 0 00
Store Equipment	54 3 1 6 00	
Accumulated Depreciation—Store Equipment		36 3 2 0 00
Accounts Payable		89 5 6 6 58
Sales Tax Payable		5 0 3 7 32
Notes Payable		50 0 0 0 00
Interest Payable		——
Unearned Rent Income		9 0 0 0 00
Employee Income Tax Payable		4 9 1 7 60
Social Security Tax Payable		4 2 4 2 62
Medicare Tax Payable		1 0 2 5 38
Medical Insurance Payable		1 3 4 4 00
Unemployment Tax Payable—State		5 8 5 60
Unemployment Tax Payable—Federal		9 1 20
Federal Income Tax Payable		——
Dividends Payable		16 0 0 0 00
Bonds Payable		15 0 0 0 00
Capital Stock—Common		80 0 0 0 00
Paid-in Capital in Excess of Par—Common		180 0 0 0 00
Capital Stock—Preferred		40 0 0 0 00

(Note: Unadjusted trial balance is continued on next page.)

22-M MASTERY PROBLEM (continued)

Ramel Corporation
Unadjusted Trial Balance (Concluded)
December 31, 20--

ACCOUNT TITLE	DEBIT	CREDIT
Paid-in Capital in Excess of Par—Preferred		
Retained Earnings		298 3 6 6 00
Dividends	64 0 0 0 00	
Income Summary		
Sales		4503 7 8 6 34
Sales Discount	11 7 8 8 72	
Sales Returns and Allowances	30 9 7 4 78	
Purchases	2996 3 6 6 16	
Purchases Discount		26 2 3 6 04
Purchases Returns and Allowances		12 3 6 8 32
Advertising Expense	32 9 7 3 80	
Cash Short and Over	3 3 76	
Credit Card Fee Expense	16 9 7 8 66	
Depreciation Expense—Office Equipment		
Depreciation Expense—Store Equipment		
Insurance Expense		
Miscellaneous Expense	84 3 7 2 60	
Payroll Taxes Expense	64 3 6 8 04	
Rent Expense	90 0 0 0 00	
Repairs Expense	12 3 0 9 98	
Salary Expense	843 0 9 6 72	
Supplies Expense		
Uncollectible Account Expense		
Utilities Expense	40 8 9 1 22	
Federal Income Tax Expense	50 0 0 0 00	
Interest Income		1 2 9 6 00
Rent Income		
Gain on Plant Assets		3 0 9 6 00
Interest Expense	7 2 0 0 00	
Loss on Plant Assets	4 8 3 0 40	
Totals	5395 6 9 9 00	5395 6 9 9 00

1., 3.

GENERAL JOURNAL

	DATE	ACCOUNT TITLE	DOC. NO.	POST. REF.	DEBIT	CREDIT	
1							1
2							2
3							3
4							4
5							5
6							6
7							7
8							8
9							9
10							10
11							11
12							12
13							13
14							14
15							15
16							16
17							17
18							18
19							19
20							20
21							21

22-M MASTERY PROBLEM (continued)

2., 4.

Allowance for Uncollectible Accounts		
Balance	320.00	
	Balance	11,020.00

Interest Receivable

Merchandise Inventory	
Balance	576,636.16
Balance	581,489.16

Supplies	
Balance	12,962.56
Balance	620.01

Prepaid Insurance	
Balance	28,000.00
Balance	4,000.00

Income Summary

Depreciation Expense—Office Equipment

Depreciation Expense—Store Equipment

Insurance Expense

Supplies Expense

Accumulated Depreciation—Office Equipment

Balance	17,420.00	
Balance	28,380.00	

Uncollectible Accounts Expense

Accumulated Depreciation—Store Equipment

Balance	36,320.00	
Balance	46,440.00	

Federal Income Tax Expense

Balance	50,000.00	
Balance	81,617.09	

Interest Payable

Interest Income

	Balance	1,296.00
	Balance	1,456.00

Unearned Rent Income

Balance	9,000.00	
Balance	3,000.00	

Rent Income

Federal Income Tax Payable

Interest Expense

Balance	7,200.00	
Balance	7,825.00	

22-M MASTERY PROBLEM (continued)

5.

Adjusted Trial Balance

ACCOUNT TITLE	DEBIT	CREDIT
Cash	55 0 3 6 50	
Petty Cash	2 5 0 00	
Accounts Receivable	251 6 9 6 50	
Allowance for Uncollectible Accounts		
Notes Receivable	8 0 0 0 00	
Interest Receivable		
Merchandise Inventory		
Supplies		
Prepaid Insurance		
Office Equipment	58 2 9 6 44	
Accumulated Depreciation—Office Equipment		
Store Equipment	54 3 1 6 00	
Accumulated Depreciation—Store Equipment		
Accounts Payable		89 5 6 6 58
Sales Tax Payable		5 0 3 7 32
Notes Payable		50 0 0 0 00
Interest Payable		
Unearned Rent Income		
Employee Income Tax Payable		4 9 1 7 60
Social Security Tax Payable		4 2 4 2 62
Medicare Tax Payable		1 0 2 5 38
Medical Insurance Payable		1 3 4 4 00
Unemployment Tax Payable—State		5 8 5 60
Unemployment Tax Payable—Federal		9 1 20
Federal Income Tax Payable		
Dividends Payable		16 0 0 0 00
Bonds Payable		15 0 0 0 00
Capital Stock—Common		80 0 0 0 00
Paid-in Capital in Excess of Par—Common		180 0 0 0 00
Capital Stock—Preferred		40 0 0 0 00

(Note: Adjusted trial balance is continued on next page.)

Adjusted Trial Balance (Concluded)

ACCOUNT TITLE	DEBIT	CREDIT
Paid-in Capital in Excess of Par—Preferred		
Retained Earnings		298 3 6 6 00
Dividends	64 0 0 0 00	
Income Summary		
Sales		4503 7 8 6 34
Sales Discount	11 7 8 8 72	
Sales Returns and Allowances	30 9 7 4 78	
Purchases	2996 3 6 6 16	
Purchases Discount		26 2 3 6 04
Purchases Returns and Allowances		12 3 6 8 32
Advertising Expense	32 9 7 3 80	
Cash Short and Over	3 3 76	
Credit Card Fee Expense	16 9 7 8 66	
Depreciation Expense—Office Equipment		
Depreciation Expense—Store Equipment		
Insurance Expense		
Miscellaneous Expense	84 3 7 2 60	
Payroll Taxes Expense	64 3 6 8 04	
Rent Expense	90 0 0 0 00	
Repairs Expense	12 3 0 9 98	
Salary Expense	843 0 9 6 72	
Supplies Expense		
Uncollectible Accounts Expense		
Utilities Expense	40 8 9 1 22	
Federal Income Tax Expense		
Interest Income		
Rent Income		
Gain on Plant Assets		3 0 9 6 00
Interest Expense		
Loss on Plant Assets	4 8 3 0 40	

22-M **MASTERY PROBLEM (continued)**

6.

	Income Statement							
								% OF SALES
Operating Revenue:								
Sales								
Less: Sales Discount								
Sales Returns and Allowances								
Net Sales								
Cost of Merchandise Sold:								
Merchandise Inventory, January 1, 20--								
Purchases								
Less: Purchases Discount								
Purchases Returns and Allowances								
Net Purchases								
Total Cost of Merchandise Available for Sale								
Less Merchandise Inventory, December 31, 20--								
Cost of Merchandise Sold								
Gross Profit								
Operating Expenses:								
Advertising Expense								
Cash Short and Over								
Credit Card Fee Expense								
Depreciation Expense—Office Equipment								
Depreciation Expense—Store Equipment								
Insurance Expense								
Miscellaneous Expense								
Payroll Taxes Expense								
Rent Expense								
Repairs Expense								
Salary Expense								
Supplies Expense								
Uncollectible Accounts Expense								
Utilities Expense								
Total Operating Expenses								
Income from Operations								
Other Revenue:								
Interest Income								
Rent Income								
Gain on Plant Assets								
Total Other Income								
Other Expenses:								
Interest Expense								
Loss on Plant Assets								
Total Other Expenses								
Net Deduction								
Net Income before Federal Income Tax								
Less Federal Income Tax Expense								
Net Income after Federal Income Tax								

7.

	Acceptable %	Actual %	Positive Result		Recommended Action if Needed
			Yes	No	
Cost of merchandise sold	Not more than 65.00%				
Gross profit on operations	Not less than 35.00%				
Total operating expenses	Not more than 30.00%				
Income from operations	Not less than 5.00%				
Net deduction from other revenue and expenses	Not more than 0.10%				
Net income before federal income tax	Not less than 4.90%				

22-M MASTERY PROBLEM (continued)

8.

Statement of Stockholders' Equity

Capital Stock—Common:											
$5.00 Par Value											
January 1, 20--, 10,000 Shares Issued											
Issued during Current Year, 6,000 Shares											
Balance, December 31, 20--, 16,000 Shares Issued											
Paid-in Capital in Excess of Par—Common:											
Balance, January 1, 20--											
Issued during Current Year											
Balance, December 31, 20--											
Capital Stock—Preferred:											
$20.00 Par Value, 5%											
January 1, 20--, 1,500 Shares Issued											
Issued during Current Year, 500 Shares											
Balance, December 31, 20--, 2,000 Shares Issued											
Retained Earnings:											
Balance, January 1, 20--											
Net Income after Federal Income Tax for 20--											
Less Dividends Declared during 20--											
Net Increase during 20--											
Balance, December 31, 20--											
Total Stockholders' Equity, December 31, 20--											

9.

Balance Sheet

Assets												
Current Assets:												
Cash												
Petty Cash												
Accounts Receivable												
Less Allowance for Uncollectible Accounts												
Notes Receivable												
Interest Receivable												
Merchandise Inventory												
Supplies												
Prepaid Insurance												
Total Current Assets												
Plant Assets:												
Office Equipment												
Less Accumulated Depreciation—Office Equipment												
Store Equipment												
Less Accumulated Depreciation—Store Equipment												
Total Plant Assets												
Total Assets												
Liabilities												
Current Liabilities:												
Accounts Payable												
Sales Tax Payable												
Notes Payable												
Interest Payable												
Unearned Rent Income												
Employee Income Tax Payable												
Social Security Tax Payable												
Medicare Tax Payable												
Medical Insurance Payable												
Unemployment Tax Payable—State												
Unemployment Tax Payable—Federal												
Federal Income Tax Payable												
Dividends Payable												
Total Current Liabilities												
Long-term Liabilities:												
Bonds Payable												
Total Long-term Liabilities												
Total Liabilities												
Stockholders' Equity												
Capital Stock—Common												
Paid-in Capital in Excess of Par—Common												
Capital Stock—Preferred												
Retained Earnings												
Total Stockholders' Equity												
Total Liabilities and Stockholders' Equity												

22-M **MASTERY PROBLEM (continued)**

10.

	Acceptable	Actual	Positive Result		Recommended Action if Needed
			Yes	No	
Working capital	Not less than $600,000.00				
Current ratio	Between 5.0 to 1 and 6.0 to 1				

11.

Statement of Cash Flows

12.

GENERAL JOURNAL

PAGE

	DATE		ACCOUNT TITLE	DOC. NO.	POST. REF.	DEBIT	CREDIT	
1								1
2								2
3								3
4								4
5								5
6								6
7								7
8								8
9								9
10								10
11								11
12								12
13								13
14								14
15								15
16								16
17								17
18								18
19								19
20								20
21								21
22								22
23								23
24								24
25								25
26								26
27								27
28								28
29								29
30								30
31								31
32								32
33								33

22-M **MASTERY PROBLEM (concluded)**

13.

GENERAL JOURNAL

PAGE _____

	DATE		ACCOUNT TITLE	DOC. NO.	POST. REF.	DEBIT	CREDIT	
1								1
2								2
3								3
4								4
5								5
6								6
7								7
8								8
9								9
10								10
11								11
12								12
13								13
14								14
15								15
16								16
17								17
18								18
19								19
20								20
21								21
22								22
23								23
24								24
25								25
26								26
27								27
28								28
29								29
30								30
31								31
32								32
33								33

Reversing entries

1. a.

GENERAL JOURNAL

PAGE 1

DATE	ACCOUNT TITLE	DOC. NO.	POST. REF.	DEBIT	CREDIT	
	Reversing Entries					1
						2
						3
						4
						5

1. b.

CASH RECEIPTS JOURNAL

PAGE 3

				1 GENERAL		3 ACCOUNTS RECEIVABLE CREDIT	4 SALES CREDIT	5 SALES TAX PAYABLE CREDIT	6 SALES DISCOUNT DEBIT	7 CASH DEBIT	
DATE	ACCOUNT TITLE	DOC. NO.	POST. REF.	DEBIT	CREDIT						
											1
											2
											3

1. a. and b.

Notes Receivable

December 31 Balance 10,000.00

Interest Receivable

December 31 Adjustment 75.00

Interest Income

December 31 Closing 75.00 | December 31 Adjustment 75.00

Cash

1. c.

Interest Income reported in 20X1 _____

Interest Income reported in 20X2 _____

22-C CHALLENGE PROBLEM (continued)

2. a.

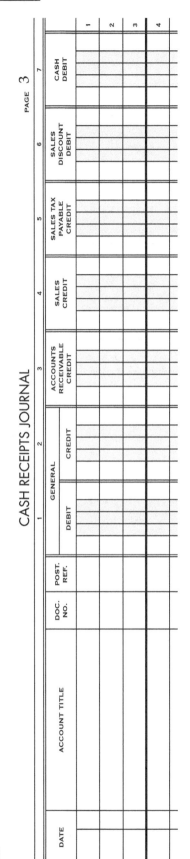

CASH RECEIPTS JOURNAL   PAGE 3

DATE	ACCOUNT TITLE	DOC. NO.	POST. REF.	GENERAL DEBIT	GENERAL CREDIT	ACCOUNTS RECEIVABLE CREDIT	SALES CREDIT	SALES TAX PAYABLE CREDIT	SALES DISCOUNT DEBIT	CASH DEBIT

2. a.

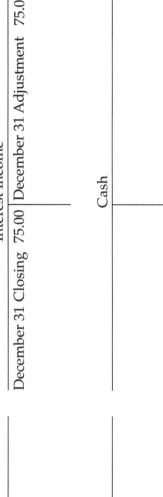

Notes Receivable		Interest Income	
December 31 Balance	10,000.00	December 31 Closing 75.00	December 31 Adjustment 75.00

Interest Receivable		Cash	
December 31 Adjustment 75.00			

2. b.

Interest Income reported in 20X1 _____

Interest Income reported in 20X2 _____

3.

_____

_____

_____

_____

_____

_____

_____

_____

_____

_____

_____

_____

_____

REINFORCEMENT ACTIVITY 3, Part B, p. 715

10.

ACCOUNT TITLE	DEBIT	CREDIT

REINFORCEMENT ACTIVITY 3, Part B (continued)

ACCOUNT TITLE	DEBIT	CREDIT

REINFORCEMENT ACTIVITY 3, Part B (continued)

11., 15.

GENERAL JOURNAL

	DATE		ACCOUNT TITLE	DOC. NO.	POST. REF.	DEBIT	CREDIT	
1								1
2								2
3								3
4								4
5								5
6								6
7								7
8								8
9								9
10								10
11								11
12								12
13								13
14								14
15								15
16								16
17								17
18								18
19								19
20								20
21								21

14.

Net Income before Federal Income Tax	–	Of the Amount Over	=	Net Income Subject to Marginal Tax Rate	×	Marginal Tax Rate	=	Marginal Income Tax
$	–	$	=	$	×		=	$

Bracket Minimum Income Tax	+	Marginal Income Tax	=	Federal Income Tax
$	+	$	=	$

Federal Income Tax	–	Taxes Already Paid	=	Amount of Adjustment
$	–	$	=	$

Name _____ Date _____ Class _____

REINFORCEMENT ACTIVITY 3, Part B (continued)

13., 16.

ACCOUNT TITLE	DEBIT	CREDIT

(Note: Adjusted trial balance is continued on next page.)

ACCOUNT TITLE	DEBIT	CREDIT

REINFORCEMENT ACTIVITY 3, Part B (continued)

17.

					% OF SALES

18.

REINFORCEMENT ACTIVITY 3, Part B (continued)

19.

20.

REINFORCEMENT ACTIVITY 3, Part B (continued)

21.

GENERAL JOURNAL   PAGE 14

	DATE		ACCOUNT TITLE	DOC. NO.	POST. REF.	DEBIT	CREDIT	
1								1
2								2
3								3
4								4
5								5
6								6
7								7
8								8
9								9
10								10
11								11
12								12
13								13
14								14
15								15
16								16
17								17
18								18
19								19
20								20
21								21
22								22
23								23
24								24
25								25
26								26
27								27
28								28
29								29
30								30
31								31
32								32
33								33

22.

ACCOUNT TITLE	DEBIT	CREDIT

REINFORCEMENT ACTIVITY 3, Part B (concluded)

23.

GENERAL JOURNAL

	DATE		ACCOUNT TITLE	DOC. NO.	POST. REF.	DEBIT	CREDIT	
1								1
2								2
3								3
4								4
5								5
6								6
7								7
8								8
9								9
10								10
11								11
12								12
13								13
14								14
15								15
16								16
17								17
18								18
19								19
20								20
21								21
22								22
23								23
24								24
25								25
26								26
27								27
28								28
29								29
30								30
31								31
32								32
33								33

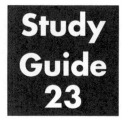

Study Guide 23

Name		Perfect Score	Your Score
	Identifying Accounting Terms	7 Pts.	
	Identifying Accounting Concepts and Practices	11 Pts.	
	Analyzing Partnership Transactions	27 Pts.	
	Total	45 Pts.	

Part One—Identifying Accounting Terms

Directions: Select the one term in Column I that best fits each definition in Column II. Print the letter identifying your choice in the Answers column.

Column I	Column II	Answers
A. distribution of net income statement	**1.** A business in which two or more persons combine their assets and skills. (p. 722)	1. _____
B. liquidation of a partnership	**2.** Each member of a partnership. (p. 722)	2. _____
C. owners' equity statement	**3.** A written agreement setting forth the conditions under which a partnership is to operate. (p. 722)	3. _____
D. partner	**4.** A partnership financial statement showing net income or loss distribution to partners. (p. 728)	4. _____
E. partnership	**5.** A financial statement that summarizes the changes in owners' equity during a fiscal period. (p. 730)	5. _____
F. partnership agreement	**6.** The process of paying a partnership's liabilities and distributing remaining assets to the partners. (p. 735)	6. _____
G. realization	**7.** Cash received from the sale of assets during liquidation of a partnership. (p. 735)	7. _____

Part Two—Identifying Accounting Concept and Practices

Directions: Place a *T* for True or an *F* for False in the Answers column to show whether each of the following statements is true or false.

Answers

1. In a partnership, it is necessary to separate reports and financial records of the business from the personal records of the partners. (p. 722)

1. _____

2. During a fiscal period, partners may take assets out of the partnership in anticipation of the net income for the period. (p. 725)

2. _____

3. Withdrawals increase the amount of a business's capital. (p. 725)

3. _____

4. The drawing accounts have normal debit balances. (p. 725)

4. _____

5. A partnership's net income or net loss may be divided unequally between the partners. (p. 728)

5. _____

6. The owners' equity statement enables business owners to determine if owners' equity is increasing or decreasing and what is causing the change. (p. 730)

6. _____

7. When a partnership goes out of business, any remaining cash is distributed to the partners according to each partner's total equity. (p. 735)

7. _____

8. Noncash assets cannot be sold for less than the recorded book value. (p. 737)

8. _____

9. The Loss on Realization account is usually included in the Other Expenses section of the chart of accounts. (p. 737)

9. _____

10. The distribution for loss or gain on realization is based on the method of distributing net income or net loss as stated in the partnership agreement. (p. 738)

10. _____

11. If there is a gain on realization, each partner's capital account is debited for the partner's share of the gain. (p. 739)

11. _____

Part Three—Analyzing Partnership Transactions

Directions: Determine in which journal each of the transactions is to be recorded. Analyze each of the following entries into debit and credit parts. Print letters (A through K) in the proper Answers columns identifying the accounts to be debited and credited.

G—General Journal; **CP**—Cash Payments Journal; **CR**—Cash Receipts Journal

Account Titles	Transactions	Journal	Debit	Credit
		Answers		
A. Accounts Payable	**1–2–3.** Partners Katlyn Chuka and Dennis Rosecrans each contribute cash and office equipment to the partnership. (p. 724)	**1.** _____	**2.** _____	**3.** _____
B. Accumulated Depreciation—Office Equipment	**4–5–6.** Dennis Rosecrans withdraws cash from the business for personal use. (p. 725)	**4.** _____	**5.** _____	**6.** _____
C. Cash	**7–8–9.** Katlyn Chuka withdraws supplies for personal use. (p. 726)	**7.** _____	**8.** _____	**9.** _____
D. Dennis Rosecrans, Capital	**10–11–12.** The partnership is liquidated, and the office equipment, costing $16,000 and having a book value of $10,000, is sold for $11,250. (p. 736)	**10.** _____	**11.** _____	**12.** _____
E. Dennis Rosecrans, Drawing	**13–14–15.** The partnership is liquidated, and the supplies valued at $400.00 are sold for $325.00. (p. 737)	**13.** _____	**14.** _____	**15.** _____
F. Gain on Realization	**16–17–18.** The partnership is liquidated, and cash is paid to all creditors for the amounts owed. (p. 738)	**16.** _____	**17.** _____	**18.** _____
G. Katlyn Chuka, Capital	**19–20–21.** A gain on realization is distributed to the partners. (p. 739)	**19.** _____	**20.** _____	**21.** _____
H. Katlyn Chuka, Drawing	**22–23–24.** A loss on realization is distributed to the partners. (p. 739)	**22.** _____	**23.** _____	**24.** _____
I. Loss on Realization	**25–26–27.** After liquidation, the remaining cash is distributed to the partners. (p. 740)	**25.** _____	**26.** _____	**27.** _____
J. Office Equipment				
K. Purchases				
L. Supplies				

Across

4. Cash received from the sale of assets during liquidation of a partnership.

5. A written agreement setting forth the conditions under which a partnership is to operate.

Down

1. A business in which two or more persons combine their assets and skills.

2. Each member of a partnership.

3. A right granted to an individual or business to sell the products or services of another, larger business within a defined geographical area.

23-1 WORK TOGETHER, p. 727

Journalizing partners' investments and withdrawals

CASH RECEIPTS JOURNAL

PAGE 7

				1 GENERAL		3 ACCOUNTS RECEIVABLE CREDIT	4 SALES CREDIT	5 SALES TAX PAYABLE CREDIT	6 SALES DISCOUNT DEBIT	7 CASH DEBIT
DATE	ACCOUNT TITLE	DOC. NO.	POST. REF.	DEBIT	CREDIT					

CASH PAYMENTS JOURNAL

PAGE 7

				1 GENERAL		3 ACCOUNTS PAYABLE DEBIT	4 PURCHASES DISCOUNT CREDIT	5 CASH CREDIT
DATE	ACCOUNT TITLE	CK. NO.	POST. REF.	DEBIT	CREDIT			

GENERAL JOURNAL

PAGE 4

	DATE		ACCOUNT TITLE	DOC. NO.	POST. REF.	DEBIT	CREDIT	
1								1
2								2
3								3
4								4
5								5
6								6
7								7
8								8
9								9
10								10
11								11
12								12
13								13
14								14
15								15
16								16
17								17
18								18
19								19
20								20
21								21
22								22
23								23
24								24
25								25
26								26
27								27
28								28
29								29
30								30
31								31
32								32

23-1 ON YOUR OWN, p. 727

Journalizing partners' investments and withdrawals

CASH RECEIPTS JOURNAL

PAGE 19

				GENERAL		ACCOUNTS RECEIVABLE CREDIT	SALES CREDIT	SALES TAX PAYABLE CREDIT	SALES DISCOUNT DEBIT	CASH DEBIT
DATE	ACCOUNT TITLE	DOC. NO.	POST. REF.	DEBIT	CREDIT					
				1	2	3	4	5	6	7

CASH PAYMENTS JOURNAL

PAGE 20

					GENERAL		ACCOUNTS PAYABLE DEBIT	PURCHASES DISCOUNT CREDIT	CASH CREDIT
DATE	ACCOUNT TITLE	CK. NO.	POST. REF.		DEBIT	CREDIT			
					1	2	3	4	5

GENERAL JOURNAL   PAGE 10

	DATE	ACCOUNT TITLE	DOC. NO.	POST. REF.	DEBIT	CREDIT	
1							1
2							2
3							3
4							4
5							5
6							6
7							7
8							8
9							9
10							10
11							11
12							12
13							13
14							14
15							15
16							16
17							17
18							18
19							19
20							20
21							21
22							22
23							23
24							24
25							25
26							26
27							27
28							28
29							29
30							30
31							31
32							32

23-2 **WORK TOGETHER, p. 734**

Preparing distribution of net income and owners' equity statements

1.

_____

_____

2.

_____

_____

_____

Preparing distribution of net income and owners' equity statements

1.

2.

23-3   WORK TOGETHER, p. 741

Liquidation of a partnership

Cash	$25,000.00
Supplies	2,400.00
Office Equipment	30,000.00
Accumulated Depreciation—Office Equipment	16,500.00
Truck	51,000.00
Accumulated Depreciation—Truck	36,600.00
Accounts Payable	2,500.00
Johanna Salo, Capital	26,800.00
Stefan Salo, Capital	26,000.00

CASH RECEIPTS JOURNAL

PAGE 7

DATE	ACCOUNT TITLE	DOC. NO.	POST. REF.	GENERAL DEBIT	GENERAL CREDIT	ACCOUNTS RECEIVABLE CREDIT	SALES CREDIT	SALES TAX PAYABLE CREDIT	SALES DISCOUNT DEBIT	CASH DEBIT
				1	2	3	4	5	6	7

CASH PAYMENTS JOURNAL

PAGE 7

				GENERAL		ACCOUNTS PAYABLE DEBIT	PURCHASES DISCOUNT CREDIT	CASH CREDIT
DATE	ACCOUNT TITLE	CK. NO.	POST. REF.	DEBIT	CREDIT			
				1	2	3	4	5

GENERAL JOURNAL

PAGE 4

DATE	ACCOUNT TITLE	DOC. NO.	POST. REF.	DEBIT	CREDIT
				1	2

23-3 ON YOUR OWN, p. 741

Liquidation of a partnership

Cash	$35,000.00
Supplies	3,000.00
Office Equipment	20,000.00
Accumulated Depreciation—Office Equipment	16,000.00
Truck	70,000.00
Accumulated Depreciation—Truck	60,000.00
Accounts Payable	16,000.00
Carlo Diaz, Capital	26,000.00
Olivia Thompson, Capital	10,000.00

CASH RECEIPTS JOURNAL

PAGE 13

DATE	ACCOUNT TITLE	DOC. NO.	POST. REF.	GENERAL DEBIT	GENERAL CREDIT	ACCOUNTS RECEIVABLE CREDIT	SALES CREDIT	SALES TAX PAYABLE CREDIT	SALES DISCOUNT DEBIT	CASH DEBIT

CASH PAYMENTS JOURNAL

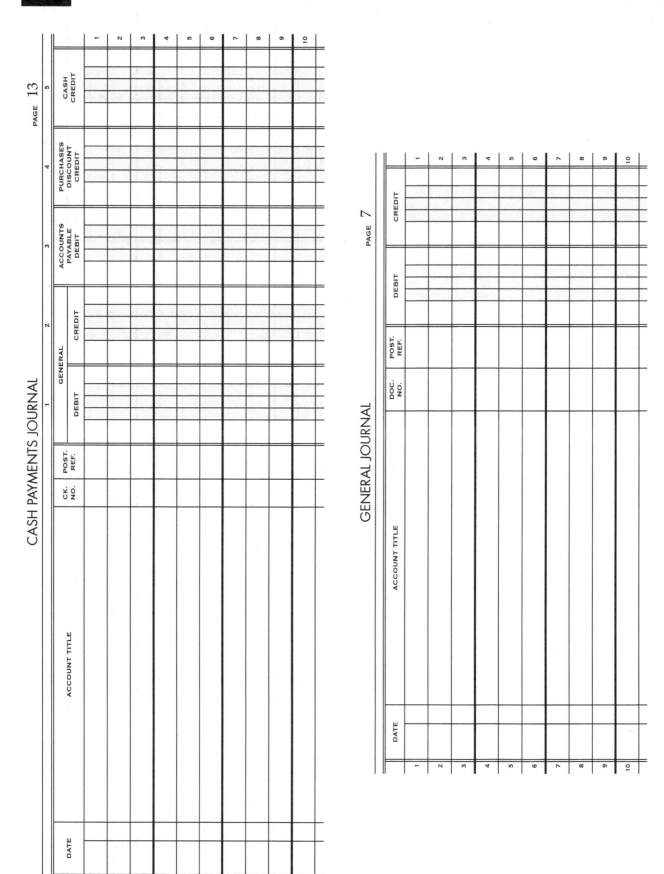

PAGE 13

| | | | | GENERAL | | ACCOUNTS PAYABLE DEBIT | PURCHASES DISCOUNT CREDIT | CASH CREDIT |
| DATE | ACCOUNT TITLE | CK. NO. | POST. REF. | DEBIT | CREDIT | | | |

GENERAL JOURNAL

PAGE 7

| DATE | ACCOUNT TITLE | DOC. NO. | POST. REF. | DEBIT | CREDIT |

23-1 APPLICATION PROBLEM (LO1, 2), p. 744

Journalizing partners' investments and withdrawals

CASH RECEIPTS JOURNAL

PAGE 9

					GENERAL		ACCOUNTS RECEIVABLE CREDIT	SALES CREDIT	SALES TAX PAYABLE CREDIT	SALES DISCOUNT DEBIT	CASH DEBIT
DATE	ACCOUNT TITLE	DOC. NO.	POST. REF.	DEBIT	CREDIT						

CASH PAYMENTS JOURNAL

PAGE 10

					GENERAL		ACCOUNTS PAYABLE DEBIT	PURCHASES DISCOUNT CREDIT	CASH CREDIT
DATE	ACCOUNT TITLE	CK. NO.	POST. REF.	DEBIT	CREDIT				

GENERAL JOURNAL PAGE 5

	DATE		ACCOUNT TITLE	DOC. NO.	POST. REF.	DEBIT	CREDIT	
1								1
2								2
3								3
4								4
5								5
6								6
7								7
8								8
9								9
10								10
11								11
12								12
13								13
14								14
15								15
16								16
17								17
18								18
19								19
20								20
21								21
22								22
23								23
24								24
25								25
26								26
27								27
28								28
29								29
30								30
31								31
32								32

23-2.1 APPLICATION PROBLEM (LO3, 4), p. 744

Preparing distribution of net income and owners' equity statements (net income)

1.

2.

Preparing an owners' equity statement (net decrease in capital)

23-3 APPLICATION PROBLEM (LO5, 6, 7), p. 745

Liquidating a partnership

CASH RECEIPTS JOURNAL

PAGE 7

						GENERAL		ACCOUNTS RECEIVABLE CREDIT	SALES CREDIT	SALES TAX PAYABLE CREDIT	SALES DISCOUNT DEBIT	CASH DEBIT
DATE	ACCOUNT TITLE	DOC. NO.	POST. REF.			DEBIT	CREDIT					
						1	2	3	4	5	6	7

CASH PAYMENTS JOURNAL

PAGE 7

				GENERAL		ACCOUNTS PAYABLE DEBIT	PURCHASES DISCOUNT CREDIT	CASH CREDIT
DATE	ACCOUNT TITLE	CK. NO.	POST. REF.	DEBIT	CREDIT			
				1	2	3	4	5

GENERAL JOURNAL

	DATE		ACCOUNT TITLE	DOC. NO.	POST. REF.	DEBIT	CREDIT	
1								1
2								2
3								3
4								4
5								5
6								6
7								7
8								8
9								9
10								10
11								11
12								12
13								13
14								14
15								15
16								16
17								17
18								18
19								19
20								20
21								21
22								22
23								23
24								24
25								25
26								26
27								27
28								28
29								29
30								30
31								31
32								32

23-M MASTERY PROBLEM (LO1, 2, 3, 4, 5, 6, 7), p. 746

Recording partners' investments and withdrawals, preparing financial statements, and liquidating a partnership

1., 4.

CASH RECEIPTS JOURNAL

PAGE 13

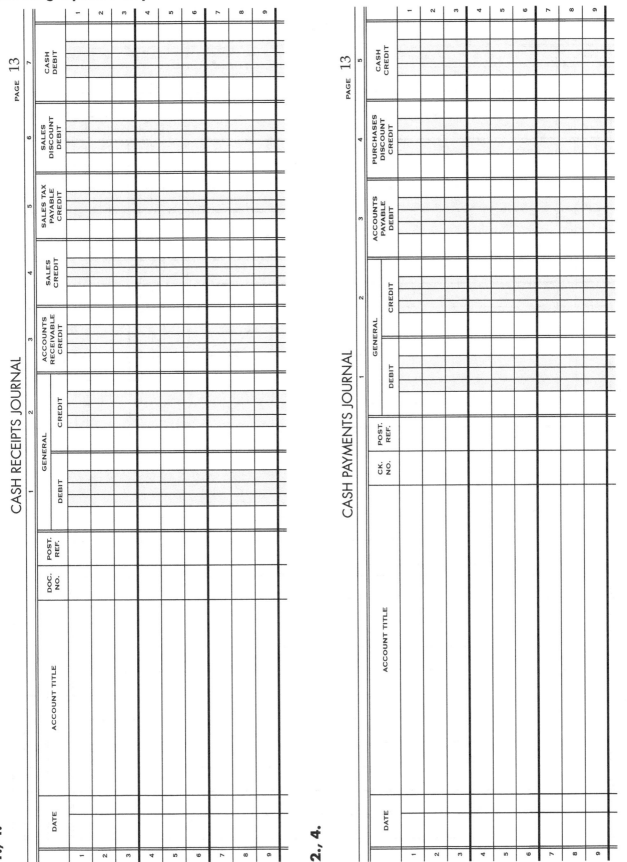

2., 4.

CASH PAYMENTS JOURNAL

PAGE 13

2., 4.

GENERAL JOURNAL

	DATE		ACCOUNT TITLE	DOC. NO.	POST. REF.	DEBIT	CREDIT	
1								1
2								2
3								3
4								4
5								5
6								6
7								7
8								8
9								9
10								10
11								11
12								12
13								13
14								14
15								15

3.

23-M **MASTERY PROBLEM (concluded)**

4.

Preparing a distribution of net income statement and an owners' equity statement with unequal distribution of net loss and additional investment

1.

2.

Name	Perfect Score	Your Score
Identifying Accounting Terms	10 Pts.	
Analyzing International and Internet Sales	10 Pts.	
Analyzing Accounts Affected by International and Internet Transactions	12 Pts.	
Total	32 Pts.	

Part One—Identifying Accounting Terms

Directions: Select the one term in Column I that best fits each definition in Column II. Print the letter identifying your choice in the Answers column.

Column I	Column II	Answers
A. bill of lading	1. Goods or services shipped out of a seller's home country to a foreign country. (p. 752)	1._____
B. commercial invoice	2. Goods or services shipped into the buyer's home country. (p. 752)	2._____
C. contract of sale	3. A document that details all the terms agreed to by seller and buyer for a sales transaction. (p. 753)	3._____
D. draft	4. A letter issued by a bank guaranteeing that a named individual or business will be paid a specified amount provided stated conditions are met. (p. 753)	4._____
E. exports	5. A receipt signed by the authorized agent of a transportation company for merchandise received that also serves as a contract for the delivery of the merchandise. (p. 754)	5._____
F. imports	6. A statement prepared by the seller of merchandise addressed to the buyer showing a detailed listing and description of merchandise sold, including prices and terms. (p. 754)	6._____
G. letter of credit	7. A written, signed, and dated order from one party ordering another party, usually a bank, to pay money to a third party. (p. 754)	7._____
H. sight draft	8. A draft payable on sight when the holder presents it for payment. (p. 754)	8._____
I. time draft	9. A draft that is payable at a fixed or determinable future time after it is accepted. (p. 757)	9._____
J. trade acceptance	10. A form signed by a buyer at the time of a sale of merchandise in which the buyer promises to pay the seller a specified sum of money, usually at a stated time in the future. (p. 758)	10._____

Part Two—Analyzing International and Internet Sales

Directions: Place a *T* for True or an *F* for False in the Answers column to show whether each of the following statements is true or false.

1. The risk of uncollected amounts is increased with international sales. (p. 753)   1. _____

2. International sales are just as simple as domestic sales. (p. 753)   2. _____

3. All transactions in the United States are covered by the same universal commercial laws and the same accounting standards. (p. 753)   3. _____

4. A draft is sometimes referred to as a bill of exchange. (p. 754)   4. _____

5. Sales taxes are normally paid only on sales to the final consumer. (p. 756)   5. _____

6. A seller generally has more assurance of receiving payment from a buyer than from a bank. (p. 758)   6. _____

7. Most businesses use trade acceptances in international sales. (p. 758)   7. _____

8. The terminal summary is used as the source document for Internet sales. (p. 761)   8. _____

9. Companies that sell on the Internet must be able to accept credit card sales. (p. 761)   9. _____

10. Credit card sales are considered the same as cash sales. (p. 762)   10. _____

Part Three—Analyzing Accounts Affected by International and Internet Transactions

Directions: Analyze each of the following transactions into debit and credit parts. Print the letter identifying your choices in the proper Answers column. Determine in which journal each of the transactions is to be recorded.

G—General Journal; **CPJ**—Cash Payments Journal; **CRJ**—Cash Receipts Journal; **S**—Sales Journal

Account Titles	Transactions	Journal	Debit	Credit
		Answers		
A. Cash	**1-2-3.** Received cash for international sale. (p. 756)	1. _____	2. _____	3. _____
B. Sales	**4-5-6.** Received a time draft for an international sale. (p. 757)	4. _____	5. _____	6. _____
C. Time Drafts Receivable	**7-8-9.** Received cash for the value of a time draft. (p. 758)	7. _____	8. _____	9. _____
	10-11-12. Recorded Internet credit card sales. (p. 762)	10. _____	11. _____	12. _____

Across

5. A form signed by a buyer at the time of a sale of merchandise in which the buyer promises to pay the seller a specified sum of money, usually at a stated time in the future.

6. A draft that is payable at a fixed or determinable future time after it is accepted.

7. A statement prepared by the seller of merchandise addressed to the buyer showing a detailed listing and description of merchandise sold, including prices and terms.

8. A draft payable on sight when the holder presents it for payment.

9. Goods or services shipped into the buyer's home country from another country.

10. A written, signed, and dated order from one party ordering another party, usually a bank, to pay money to a third party.

Down

1. Goods or services shipped out of a seller's home country to another country.

2. A letter issued by a bank guaranteeing that a named individual or business will be paid a specified amount provided stated conditions are met.

3. A document that details all the terms agreed to by seller and buyer for a sales transaction.

4. A receipt signed by the authorized agent of a transportation company for merchandise received that also serves as a contract for the delivery of the merchandise.

24-1 WORK TOGETHER, p. 760

Journalizing international sales transactions

1., 2.

CASH RECEIPTS JOURNAL

PAGE 6

DATE	ACCOUNT TITLE	DOC. NO.	POST. REF.	GENERAL DEBIT	GENERAL CREDIT	ACCOUNTS RECEIVABLE CREDIT	SALES CREDIT	SALES DISCOUNT DEBIT	CASH DEBIT
									1
									2
									3

1.

GENERAL JOURNAL

PAGE

DATE	ACCOUNT TITLE	DOC. NO.	POST. REF.	DEBIT	CREDIT	
						1
						2
						3
						4
						5
						6
						7
						8
						9
						10

Journalizing international sales transactions

1., 2.

CASH RECEIPTS JOURNAL

PAGE

					GENERAL		ACCOUNTS RECEIVABLE CREDIT	SALES CREDIT	SALES DISCOUNT DEBIT	CASH DEBIT	
DATE	ACCOUNT TITLE	DOC. NO.	POST. REF.	DEBIT	CREDIT						
				1	2	3	4	5	6		
											1
											2
											3

1.

GENERAL JOURNAL

PAGE

DATE	ACCOUNT TITLE	DOC. NO.	POST. REF.	DEBIT	CREDIT	
						1
						2
						3
						4
						5
						6
						7
						8
						9
						10

24-2 WORK TOGETHER, p. 763

Journalizing Internet sales transactions

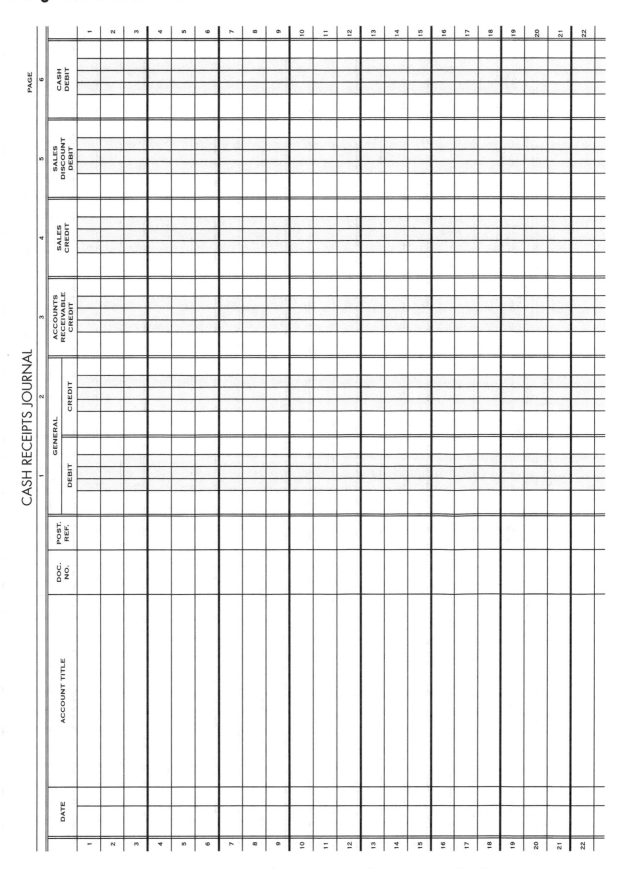

CASH RECEIPTS JOURNAL

							GENERAL		ACCOUNTS RECEIVABLE CREDIT	SALES CREDIT	SALES DISCOUNT DEBIT	CASH DEBIT
DATE	ACCOUNT TITLE	DOC. NO.	POST. REF.		DEBIT	CREDIT						

PAGE 6

Journalizing Internet sales transactions

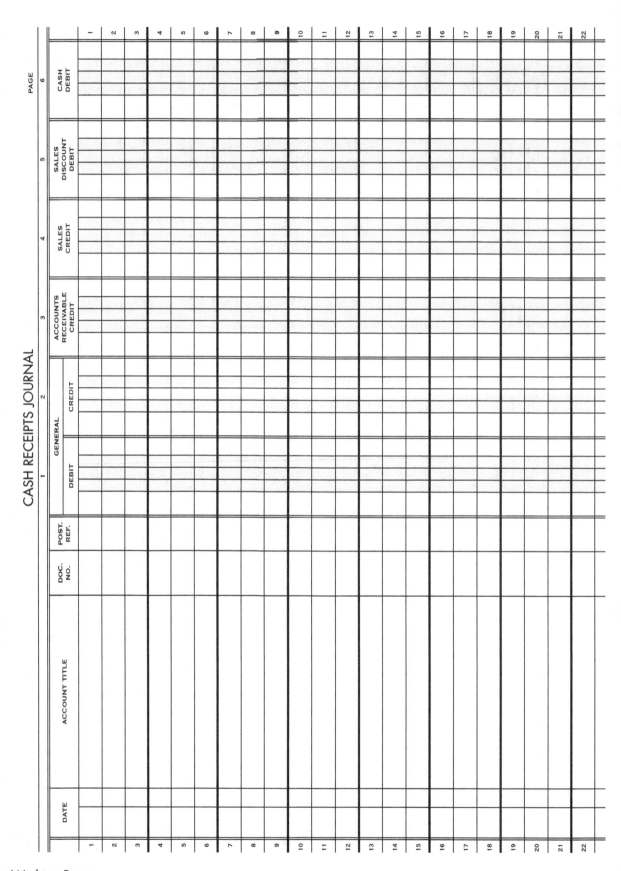

CASH RECEIPTS JOURNAL

PAGE 6

DATE	ACCOUNT TITLE	DOC. NO.	POST. REF.	GENERAL DEBIT	GENERAL CREDIT	ACCOUNTS RECEIVABLE CREDIT	SALES CREDIT	SALES DISCOUNT DEBIT	CASH DEBIT

24-1 **APPLICATION PROBLEM (LO4, 5), p. 767**

Journalizing international sales transactions

1., 2.

CASH RECEIPTS JOURNAL PAGE 6

DATE	ACCOUNT TITLE	DOC. NO.	POST. REF.	GENERAL DEBIT	GENERAL CREDIT	ACCOUNTS RECEIVABLE CREDIT	SALES CREDIT	SALES DISCOUNT DEBIT	CASH DEBIT
1									
2									
3									
4									
5									
6									

1.

GENERAL JOURNAL PAGE

DATE	ACCOUNT TITLE	DOC. NO.	POST. REF.	DEBIT	CREDIT
1					
2					
3					
4					
5					
6					
7					
8					
9					
10					

Journalizing Internet sales transactions

1., 2.

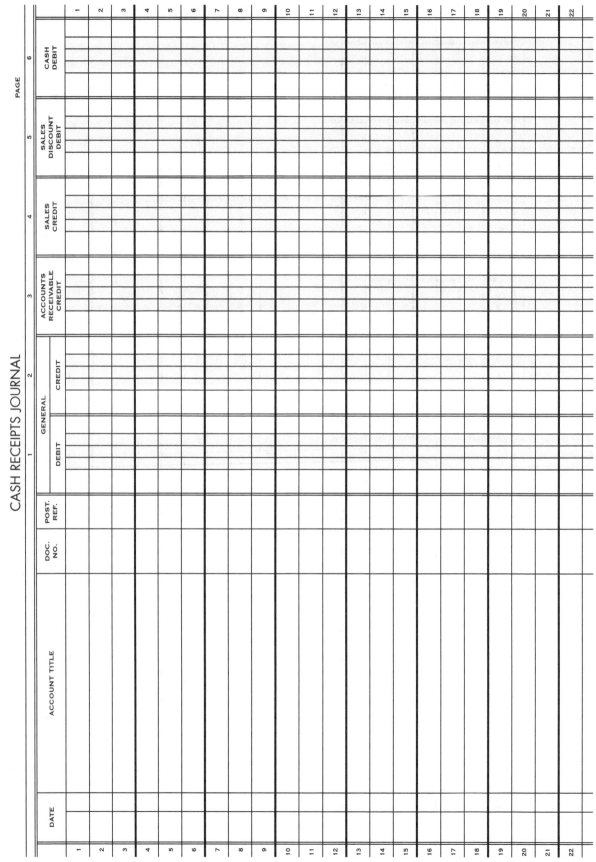

CASH RECEIPTS JOURNAL

PAGE 6

	DATE	ACCOUNT TITLE	DOC. NO.	POST. REF.	GENERAL DEBIT 1	GENERAL CREDIT 2	ACCOUNTS RECEIVABLE CREDIT 3	SALES CREDIT 4	SALES DISCOUNT DEBIT 5	CASH DEBIT 6	
1											1
2											2
3											3
4											4
5											5
6											6
7											7
8											8
9											9
10											10
11											11
12											12
13											13
14											14
15											15
16											16
17											17
18											18
19											19
20											20
21											21
22											22

24-M MASTERY PROBLEM (LO4, 5, 6), p. 768

Recording international and Internet sales

1., 2.

CASH RECEIPTS JOURNAL

PAGE 6

DATE	ACCOUNT TITLE	DOC. NO.	POST. REF.	GENERAL DEBIT	GENERAL CREDIT	ACCOUNTS RECEIVABLE CREDIT	SALES CREDIT	SALES DISCOUNT DEBIT	CASH DEBIT

1.

GENERAL JOURNAL

PAGE

DATE	ACCOUNT TITLE	DOC. NO.	POST. REF.	DEBIT	CREDIT

24-C CHALLENGE PROBLEM (LO4), p. 768

Recording international sales and converting foreign currency

1., 2.

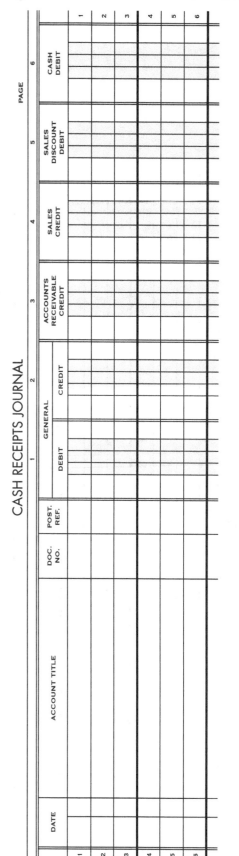

CASH RECEIPTS JOURNAL

Exchange Rate _____

U.S. Dollars _____

Date _____   Amount _____